GARDENING *with*

ANTIQUE PLANTS

DAVID STUART

conran
OCTOPUS

CONTENTS

THE STORY OF ANTIQUE PLANTS

In 1896, an American writer, George H. Ellwanger, wrote ecstatically of his own, and neighbouring, gardens in Rochester, New York: 'You would know by the scent of the lilies that summer was here. How fragrant the censer of June! How profuse the scent of blossoming vegetation! – odors not alone from myriads of plants, but breathing from orchards, hedges, and thickets, rising from woods and hillsides, blown from meadows and pastures...' He admired, too, the gardens of 'tumble down farmsteads' where the loveliest American flowers and the loveliest of Europe too filled the air with perfume. But he, like many of his European counterparts, was beginning to regret the loss of the very flowers of those old farmstead gardens, all being speedily replaced by new discoveries, and the then new 'bedding' style of gardening. He had a long list of plants that he sorely missed: snowdrops, the old double daffodils, imperials (he meant *Fritillaria imperialis*), muscaris, larkspurs, campanulas of all sorts, bachelors' buttons, monkshoods, double white poppies, sweet clover, snow pink, white phloxes, dicentras, sweet Williams (grown in Europe since the sixteenth century), tall yellow tulips, tradescantias, sweet peas, valerians, madonna lilies (the same as those grown in the most ancient gardens of Mesopotamia, thousands of years ago), white and purple stocks, lily of the valley, briar rose (which the first Dutch settlers brought to Manhattan), white daylily (he probably meant hosta), tiger lilies, dahlias, hollyhocks (grown in New England by 1621) and even sunflowers.

This book is the story of these and many other antique plants, of their origins, of how they have been used in gardens and how the many that can still be grown may be used today. It covers all sorts of species, from wild flowers native to North America or Europe to plants gathered in some foreign clime and grown here as exotics.

Opposite: *Canarina canariense*, the Canary Island bellflower. This one, painted for the *Botanical Magazine* in the late eighteenth century, still makes a charming perennial climber in frost-free gardens.

Left: At the height of their popularity in the eighteenth century, uniformly coloured tulips were called 'mothers'; the colour breaks that transformed them into gorgeous 'flamed' or 'feathered' sorts were caused by a virus which affected different layers of the petals in different ways.

Above: *Kennedia coccinea,* painted for the *Botanical Magazine,* can make a spectacular antique climber for warm gardens, or for conservatories.

WHAT IS AN ANTIQUE?

In gardening terms, an 'antique' is anything over a hundred years old. This is but the tiniest slice of time for plants in evolutionary terms, while it is an age for many garden flowers or fruits, bred as the latest thing, the most brilliant or the highest yielding. It is quite long enough to see them go out of fashion, and then become extinct.

In most important groups of garden plants like roses or apples, carnations or crocuses, new varieties have continued to appear throughout the garden history of the species. You will find in these pages plant varieties which are still commercially available, but which relate to a specific epoch in the garden. In some genera (apples, roses, vines, irises, tulips and so on, each of which easily merits a book to itself), there are still huge numbers of varieties around. While not all are antique, and fewer still 'deep' antiques from the very beginning of gardening, the treatment here is necessarily brief; I have chosen mostly species and varieties that I have grown and liked, and which will associate well with other plants in this book.

Of course, almost every pure plant species is an antique, and what grows in the garden now is exactly the same as what might have grown in medieval gardens, or in the wilds of Afghanistan, or on the banks of the Mekong River long ages before gardening even began. After all, the species might be tens of thousands, or even millions of years old. For the purposes of this book, wild species are 'aged' by the date when they were first cultivated in the documented garden; so, for instance, many orchid species, having grown for millions of years among the damp branches of Amazonian jungles, are here 'nineteenth-century' because that is when they began to be grown in European and American glasshouses – even though some of them may, perhaps much earlier, have been used by Native Americans.

But are there really many antique garden plants left? The answer is yes, there are some astonishing, and ancient, survivals. Your garden, whatever its size, can grow at least some of the flowers found in Dutch flower paintings of the seventeenth century; tulips from sixteenth-century Constantinople; or the enchanting double-flowered chelidonium found in a hedgerow by the botanist John Rea in the 1630s. You can still find the strange little 'Plymouth strawberry', discovered in that town in 1632; it was worn on ladies' bodices for decoration and is so odd that it has always intrigued just enough gardeners to keep it alive. You can grow the 'Cross of Jerusalem' (*Lychnis chalcedonica*), probably brought to Western European gardens by returning Crusaders, or have roses from ancient Rome, or squashes that were known in Central America in the fifteenth century.

There are certainly plenty of plants to make an enchanting antique garden. The aim of this book is to help you find some of the loveliest antiques, and to show how they can be grown in contemporary gardens. By that I mean gardens which are not museum pieces, but which are, nevertheless, filled with the beauty and romance of ancient plants.

Below: A Victorian seed catalogue from Benary, a German firm which still exists, showing contemporary varieties of garden pea.

PLATE VI.
Painted & Published as the Act directs by the Author G.Brookshaw July 1ˢᵗ 1805.

Right: Prize-winning gooseberries, often bred by artisan enthusiasts, reached prodigious sizes; the tiny leaves shown here may reflect the scale of the fruit. Many varieties with these colours and textures can still be grown.

Opposite: A rose from the hand of Redouté; though this variety may be lost, 'Tuscany Superb' makes a close and easily grown substitute.

THE ROMANCE OF ANTIQUE PLANTS

For me, the real fascination of many antique plants is the way in which so many are so intimately bound up with the history of conquests and wars, of trade, of peace and plenty, and of social change. It's hard not to find a bowl of cherries from your own garden more romantic when you know how much they were valued by Mithridates, King of Pontus, a ruler so proud of his great knowledge that he wrote one of the first plant treatises, in the first century BC. When his kingdom was destroyed by the Roman general Lucullus, the cherries, unknown to the Romans, were carried back to Italy and the trees were one of the treasures displayed at Lucullus's subsequent 'triumph'.

By the same token it is difficult, when planting a tulip bulb, not to think of the stories of their introduction to the West. In one version, an ambassador at the court of Suleiman the Magnificent is supposed to have sent seeds back to Vienna in 1554. The first tulip from this seed flowered in a private garden in Augsburg in 1559.

Another version of the story concerns a cargo of Turkish bulbs that apparently arrived in Antwerp in 1562. The burghers of that great city, not knowing what the bulbs were, tried cooking them. Finding them not to their taste, they threw the remaining uncooked ones on to a midden, where a few of them subsequently flowered and caused a storm of interest. If this story is true, however, the bulbs must have been wild species or unfashionable varieties, for choice Turkish garden tulips were far too expensive in Constantinople to be bought by the sackful, even by the rich merchants of Antwerp.

Even that modern staple of late summer cottage gardens, the Japanese anemone (*Anemone hupehensis*), has drama; the form with purple semi-double flowers was discovered in 1844, growing on tombs on the ramparts of Shanghai, and the great collector Robert Fortune almost lost his life to pirates as he attempted to bring the plants home.

FLORISTS AND COLLECTORS

Plant stories are also bound up with the stories of ordinary and forgotten gardeners, from one Mistress Tuggy, who in Elizabethan London was following her late husband's example by selecting auricula seedlings so pretty that she gets a mention in John Parkinson's great garden book of 1629, *Paradisi in Sole Paradisus Terrestris*, to another of Parkinson's contacts, 'my good friend Vincent Sion'. None of Mistress Tuggy's auriculas seem to have survived, whereas the old double narcissus called 'Van Sion', after Vincent, is still delighting admirers of daffodils.

These two gardeners were among the first 'florists'; not florists in the way that we now use the word – of people who sell flowers – but gardeners obsessed enough with their favourite types of plant to sow endless seed, nurture the seedlings, grow them until they flowered and then save but two or three of the most enchanting of the results. Some well-documented florists are still memorialized in plant names, like the ones named 'Sam Barlow'. Mr Barlow (1824–88), from modest beginnings, became a partner in a bleach works at Rochdale in Lancashire. Selecting new forms of garden flower that would win prizes on the show bench was his hobby, and he was so good at it that he became known as 'King of the Northern Florists', particularly for his auriculas: he grew 500 seedlings every season, keeping only the two or three most beautiful. He still has a gorgeous florists' tulip named after him (not, however, of his breeding, and not in commerce) and a garden pink, maroon centred and smelling of cloves and lemon zest.

Mr Barlow, who was educated and eventually became prosperous, was among the 'stars' of his day. The push forward in the creation of new varieties, or even of whole groups of varieties, sometimes came from wealthy collectors or, in the late nineteenth century, from big nurseries. But more often it came from unnamed and now totally forgotten individual 'florists'. Most of them were members of the manufacturing classes, usually urban; they grew the plants for showing at local meetings and took the best plants of all to larger shows in the big cities. The rewards were not just aesthetic; good 'show' plants won money and found a ready market for cuttings and offsets.

Almost any plant in the garden could be adopted as a florists' flower, though obviously ones which held a lot of genetic diversity, or which could be crossed with related species, were the best choices. Important antique florists' groups included auriculas, violas, tulips, roses, hyacinths, anemones. Modern equivalents are irises, daylilies, ericas and so on. But genetic diversity was apparent among fruits, too, so some easily grown fruits were bred in backyards and had clubs devoted to showing the results of breeding: the gooseberry was a popular 'subject'.

However, as with modern intensely bred groups, what made the difference between new 'varieties' became smaller and smaller, until the varieties were scarcely distinguishable. As now, the fashion for a particular group lost momentum, and the florists' attention then shifted elsewhere in pursuit of some other ideal. Huge numbers of plants were thrown out, and the ones that somehow survived were confused with others that looked almost similar. Even those became infected with viruses, lost vigour, lost their names and retreated into the obscurity shared with their breeders. Some old florists' societies still exist, from the tiny and sadly diminishing Paisley Florists' Club (founded in 1795 for the competitive showing of anemones, pinks, carnations, hyacinths and tulips, though now specializing in overweight vegetables) to the Wakefield Tulip Society, formed probably in the early nineteenth century and still having annual shows of old 'flamed' tulips.

Opposite: Nineteenth-century variants of Swiss chard, some with deep ruby stems, others with 'savoyed' foliage; comparable forms can still be found.

Below: Although the name of this fine narcissus (painted by Redouté in the nineteenth century) can no longer be traced, similar dark-cupped varieties are still grown.

Gardeners at the other end of the social scale became equally passionate about plant variation and the creation of new varieties; the aristocratic Thomas Knight – brother and eventual heir to the rakish Richard, whose obsessive interest in classical civilization made him a leading propagandist for the nineteenth-century developments in the landscape style, of which more later – spent his time (and money) quietly at Downton Castle in Shropshire, writing on horticulture and breeding new strawberries from the exciting American species arriving in Europe. He was responsible for huge numbers of publications, all of which survive. None of his strawberries do.

But florists were gardeners who did not stray beyond their own fences. Some garden plants, however, demanded much more adventurousness from their devotees, and risk was had in plenty by some of the great plant hunters, from the Tradescants, father and son, to the nineteenth-century collectors like David Douglas and Robert Fortune. John Tradescant the Elder (1570–1638) journeyed to Europe several times, even visiting the island of Cos, from which he collected the first 'Cos' lettuces to be seen in Europe. Although Cos lettuces in fact originated in ancient Egypt, Tradescant's name for them has stuck. He went on to explore the furthest points of Russia, from where he brought back the first larch tree to be seen in western Europe. John the Younger (1608–62) was even more daring, making the trip to North America three, perhaps four times and bringing back the first American asters.

However, the Golden Age of collecting from the Americas was the early decades of the nineteenth century, and perhaps the most influential collector was David Douglas. Financed by what became the Royal Horticultural Society, he explored the then unimaginably remote west coast of America, the Rockies and the central states. Often enduring appalling conditions, he collected immensely important plants, from the tiny *Penstemon scouleri* to the vast *Sequoia sempervirens*, via camassias, flowering currants, *Garrya elliptica* and many more conifers, including the 'Douglas fir' (*Pseudotsuga menziesii*). On a final trip, he visited Hawaii. He died there, and was found, mangled, at the bottom of a staked pit that should have caught wild cattle. His last collections were beside him.

In the East, trampled almost bare by the number of collectors after rhododendrons, roses and rare alpines, one of the most notable collectors was Robert Fortune. By 1847 he was busily buying up all the interesting camellias (as well as moutan peonies and dozens of other good plants) from Chinese nurseries, private gardens and wild hillsides. Like David Douglas and many other collectors (and indeed, many head gardeners of the time), Fortune was a Scot, born in Berwickshire in 1812. He eventually became a gardener at the Edinburgh Botanic Garden; from there he moved to Chiswick House, in West London, where he looked after the tropical collection. Whilst he was in the capital, China was opened to foreigners and, following the Treaty of Nanking in 1842, Fortune was sent out to find as many good garden plants as he could.

For a man who had never travelled out of Britain, and who had hated the sea passage from Leith to London, this must have been a daunting prospect. It was nevertheless a dazzling success. In spite of thieves, beggars, conmen, pirates, obstructive mandarins and brushes with various oriental diseases, Fortune finally returned to London loaded with gorgeous plants. Many of these were brought back in Wardian cases (see page 149), and many plants that would otherwise not have survived the long and arduous journey were soon in full bloom at Chiswick. Fortune eventually retired, wrote best-selling memoirs and died at home.

Opposite: Hyacinths with dense heads of flowers were favourites in Victorian bedding schemes, and were bred to make intense sheets of colour. Older varieties were often much more lax.

FINDING OLD FLOWERS

However exciting it is to gather together a collection of antique flowers and make a garden with them, even more exciting is the hunt for forgotten flowers still hanging on in cottage gardens or abandoned patches by the wayside. But don't underestimate the difficulties. The chances of finding a lovely old plant, whether daylily, carnation or apple tree, still with a mouldering (and decipherable) label attached to it are minute.

To make matters worse, it is very hard to identify old garden flowers from original sources. Descriptions in eighteenth-century or earlier garden books are almost never sufficiently detailed, or well enough illustrated, to allow precise identification. Woodcuts (when available) are some help, but not much, and herbarium specimens are virtually useless – every herbarium seems to have sheets of brown pressed tulips, brown carnations and brown auriculas. Though it is fascinating to see late seventeenth-century garden flowers in the flesh, none of the specimens is ever much use in matching with the living plant that the eager gardener hopes to clinch as an ancient survivor.

The most that can be said for some garden flowers, including a number in this book, is that they clearly belong to old 'groups', say the 'pheasant's eye' pinks, the 'rennet' apples or the 'tazetta' narcissi. They can never be referred to with any certainty by an old variety name. Indeed, the plant may not have had one, if it was just a local variant or never in commerce. For most gardeners, perhaps, that doesn't matter; as long as a plant clearly belongs to an antique group, then it should be welcomed into the garden. There have, though, been attempts at crossing some of the best antiques to give them modern attributes, like the roses that almost look like old ones, but flower all year, or laced pinks that do the same. Such plants have their advantages, but have almost always also lost much of their charm.

Opposite: The 1830 catalogue of the London nurserymen Loddiges lists 40 species of *Dianthus*, without even beginning on the immense numbers of cultivated varieties.

Left: More plates from the Benary catalogue; many of the squash varieties can still be found, and can be grown in most gardens.

GROWING ANTIQUE PLANTS

Although we can pinpoint the date when many plants appeared in gardens, or garden literature, for the first time, none need be rigorously related to a particular place or historical time. The deliberate use of antique plants is a recent phenomenon which doesn't need to be treated as an academic exercise; the plants can be grown for your own pleasure in a garden with no past, or in a single pot on the windowsill. They are for everyone, not just the owners of historical acres or grand houses. This book suggests ways of growing them which will look beautiful, crop well and smell delicious.

They can also lead on to other interests which can help in the search for antique plants, whether that is to visit other gardens or the collections of antique plants already scattered through Europe and America, or to investigate the existing garden documentation, vital sources of information like old plant catalogues, lists, pictures and books. It is an exciting field for, now that so much of the world's native flora has been discovered, the past is the new frontier.

THE COTTAGE GARDEN

It is an appealing idea: pushing open a village gate to find a garden heady with perfume, buzzing with bees, with opulent rows of beans and marigolds, old cabbage roses and caterpillar-free cabbages, and with a rickety seat under an ancient but still heavily laden apple tree. By the cottage are planted beds of pinks or of old auriculas or 'cottage' tulips, thrown out of the garden of the 'big house' but treasured here for their smell, or for the shape or markings of their petals.

Little is known about how medieval peasants in Italy, or Elizabethan ones in England, or even those of seventeenth-century France lived. Serious interest in how the owners or tenants of cottages existed, let alone gardened, only really began in the early nineteenth century, and it wasn't until the 1850s, when some sophisticated and wealthy gardeners' taste for the very latest flowers began to get jaded, that a few started to rummage in cottage gardens for flowers that they remembered, or had read of, from the past.

Left: Elizabethan gardens were bright with all forms and colours of tagetes; here they are mixed with nicotianas, rudbeckias and others, and still make a pretty planting for cottage gardens. Above: Persian ranunculus are easy to grow, and flower at the same time as the later tulips; a mix of the two can give a spectacular show.

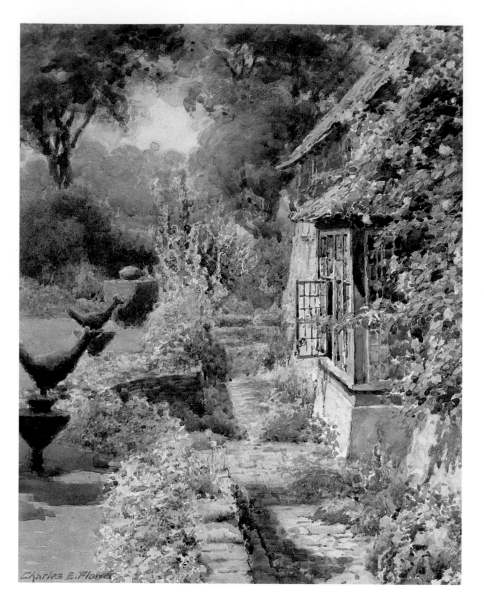

Above: Hollyhocks, roses around the window, pinks, campanulas in among the paving and topiary birds make up this cottage-garden idyll, painted by Charles Edwin Flower in 1871 in the gardens of Kings Manor, Berkshire.

Though many cottagers turned out to be as interested in the new as anyone else, some cottage gardens proved still to contain splendid old plants. All sorts of interesting specimens turned up, from the ancient double yellow wallflower found by the Reverend Harpur Crewe (and which now bears his name), double forms of campion and campanula, old 'flaked' carnations and pinks, curiosities like the 'rose' plantain, ancient real roses, antique daffodils, to old fruit and vegetable varieties.

These discoveries fuelled the cottage-garden ideal, one that is still powerfully alive. Now, not only are old flowers ardently collected and nurtured, but historic gardens are also being rebuilt and replanted in countries that have sufficient interest and resources. In general, though, 'historic' also means 'grand' and usually 'well-documented'. But small gardens must have been beautiful too, though they can be glimpsed only occasionally in poetry, paintings or ancient garden books.

The 'cottage style' of gardening sometimes attempts historical authenticity and indeed, as it is seen now – with a romantic 'muzz' of plants, given form by paths, lavender or box hedges, self-sown plants of aquilegia or 'Jacobs's ladder', perhaps some topiary, certainly some old fruit trees – it may bear some resemblance to how old small gardens looked. Certainly, British and American garden writers in the 1880s could have heard about the countryside gardens of their grandparents. Gardens can easily remain without rebuilding for almost a hundred years, so some late eighteenth-century cottage gardens were probably still in existence. But for anything earlier, gardeners have to rely on the garden books that began to appear towards the end of the seventeenth century, written for the minor gentry.

Important for the cottage-garden movement were works like the poetical *Paradisi in Sole Paradisus Terrestris*, written by John Parkinson in 1629, the rather more modest *The Scots Gardener*, written by John Reid in 1683, and the long sequence of editions of *The Gardener's Dictionary* by Philip Miller, starting in 1731. In all of them, and especially in Reid's book, the way of integrating formal layout with luscious planting, of mixing flowers with fruit and vegetables, is splendidly set out. From these books, too, come inspiring gardening ideas: smothering gateways with jasmine and honeysuckle; turning the corners in paths with the help of a topiary emphasis; having pots of 'greens' (a term which meant almost any tender exotic newly imported from Italy, China or America) as the centrepieces to flowerbeds. Yet in many parts of the western world 'cottagers' were desperately poor, so thoughts of gardening anything more than vegetables for their own consumption would have seemed absurd. Perhaps, then, the modern image of cottage gardening is really a much faded picture of small manor-house gardens of long ago.

Whatever its origins, the cottage garden makes an exciting and productive way of combining a wide range of antique plants, satisfying around almost any sort of house, yet giving as much resonance of the past as any garden needs. Better, planting a cottage garden is fun. This is largely because there is no set way of doing it: it can vary from something kept reasonably trim, with topiary, brickwork paths and antique flowers, to a floriferous tangle, unrestrained, perfumed and colourful, cheerfully combining cabbages, morning glories, jasmine and dahlias.

Height can be given by fruit trees, and if you worry about bringing thieves in after apples, plant crabs, myrobalans, medlars or filberts – all delicious crops that will appeal to you, but probably not to them. Porches and doorways are always worth emphasizing; use some of the climbers detailed later in this chapter, or those suggested for the rose garden (see page 102). For somewhere to escape from the kitchen or the phone, give the garden a rustic arbour, either as a feature in its own right or attached to the side of the garage, barn, garden shed or privy. Many companies sell ready-made metal and wire-work ones, but something suitably rustic is easily made from scrap timber, or wood and poles. In the nineteenth century, arbours were commonly covered with runner beans, climbing French beans or climbing squashes and marrows. They need to be deep enough to give shade to the seat on a hot afternoon.

Paths in cottage gardens give form to the planting, and often look best when going directly from one point to another. To give extra emphasis to the line, edge them with box or clipped ivy. Brick makes a good surface, though flagstones or stone cobbles look even better. Hard surfaces like these are more easily swept clean of cabbage stalks and rose petals than is gravel. Lawns and grass paths are not part of a cottage garden, unless you are lucky enough to have an orchard.

The boundary fence or hedge is an important part of the design, keeping the world at bay and giving structure to the plot. Drape rails and palings with climbers, or give the hedge a topiary flourish. If you live in the house full-time, give yourself a 'florists corner' for some of the enchanting old flowers that look good in their own pots (old tulips, laced polyanthuses or show auriculas). But best of all, ensure that you have a sitting place for a summer evening, amid the heady perfumes of mignonette, stocks, nicotianas, jasmine and honeysuckle.

Below: Brilliant anemones like this have been illuminating Western gardens since the sixteenth century, and Middle Eastern ones for much longer. This one dates from about 1800.

BULBS AND PERENNIALS

Among the bulbs and perennials of the cottage garden are some of the most cherished of all garden antiques. Some are to be found in every sales outlet; others have to be sought out. Some can be so vigorous that they will take over the garden; others need coddling if they are to flourish, but provide enormous rewards if they do.

Although a small cottage garden could easily be made using only plants from this chapter, you could try adding some roses, a topiary box or two and a fruit tree. Cottage gardens can easily provide interest for most of the year, and be brimming with flowers from spring into late summer.

Acanthus ACANTHUS, BEARS' BREECHES

Only two of this handsome genus are antique garden plants. But they have probably been popular since ancient Greece, and certainly since Roman times. Both *Acanthus mollis* and the frillier *A. spinosus* were still widely grown in European

Above: The leaves of *Acanthus mollis* have inspired designers from the architects of Ancient Greece, where they were the source for the curling foliage at the top of Corinthian columns, to William Morris. The plant makes a dramatic focal point in the cottage plot.

Right: In a cottage border dark maroon hollyhocks look good behind roses such as 'Ispahan' and 'Maiden's Blush': fill in the planting with fennels, the taller campanulas and white tree lupins.

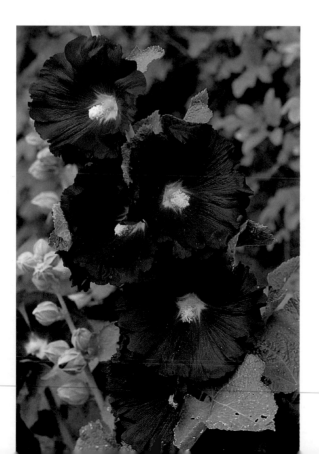

gardens by the mid 1500s, though by 1754 they were thought worthy only of collectors' gardens.

In 1870, William Robinson, the English champion of wild flowers, extolled their virtues for the wild garden. Don't be put off; their extravagant foliage looks good in cottage ones, especially by a doorway or beneath an ancient apple tree.

Alcea HOLLYHOCK

Hollyhocks have been in cultivation in Europe and Asia for so long that they have lost any connection with a known wild species. But the great age of the hollyhock really began in Britain and North America in about the 1840s. There were many famous breeders, though only an Englishman named Chater is remembered; his double-flowered varieties can still be found. In the cottage gardens of Europe and America, they were grown at the back of borders, often against walls, where the tall flower spikes were easily held in place and the basal leaves covered by other flowers. For an eighteenth-century look, grow the pink-flowered marshmallow (*Althaea officinalis*), once planted in cottage borders for late summer colour.

Anemone ANEMONE

Of the 120 or so species, all from the northern hemisphere, the best have been in the garden for many centuries. For early spring, the 'St Bavo' forms (*Anemone pavonina*) have been grown in Europe since the sixteenth century and were in Turkish gardens probably much earlier. Sir Thomas Hanmer, a famous seventeenth-century gardener, grew them mixed with the latest fraxinellas, new American tradescantias and English primroses and daffodils. Copy that planting in your garden to give you flowers from early spring to midsummer.

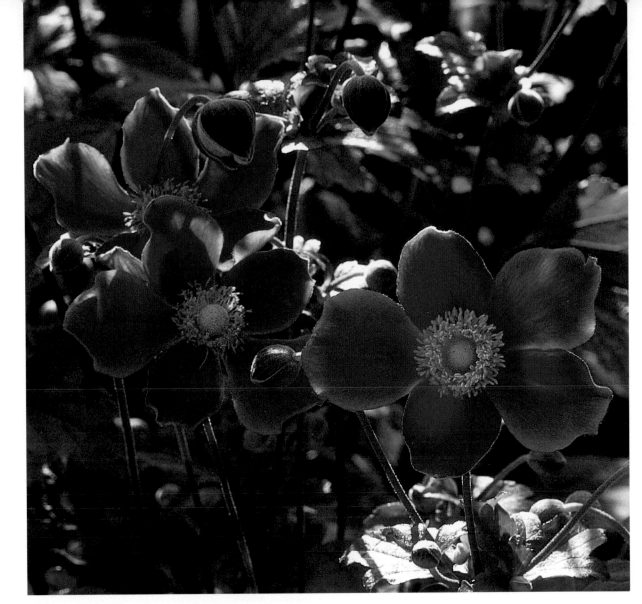

Right: Introduced from the Far East, *Anemone hupenhensis* 'Splendens' was an essential feature of the mid to late nineteenth-century cottage border

Below: A semi-double form of white *Anemone nemorosa*, popular in the eighteenth century, is useful for brightening shady areas in a cottage garden.

Anemone coronaria is the 'de Caen' anemone; wild from the Mediterranean region to central Asia, it was first taken up in Western Europe by the florists of the French city after whom it is named. No early sorts survive, but double types available now make excellent substitutes for eighteenth-century gardens. They had been grown earlier, for in the early 1600s both types were crossed, with the handsome *Anemone* x *fulgens* the result. Of the richest vermilion and scarlet, it's still available.

For summer and autumn borders, grow *Anemone hupehensis* (*A.* x 'Japonica' and other varieties) from China and Japan. All reached the West after 1844, though they had been oriental garden plants for centuries before. Soft pink and perfect white forms were appearing in the 1860s.

Aquilegia COLUMBINE, AQUILEGIA

The fifty or so species come from all over the northern hemisphere. Before the mid-seventeenth century, only one (*Aquilegia vulgaris*) was grown in Europe. Variable in the wild, it flowers in violet, white or red, and is sometimes bicoloured. Single columbines can often be seen in medieval paintings and illuminations. They are still available.

One medieval painting shows a plant very similar to today's *Aquilegia vulgaris* 'Adelaide Addison', so that form may be hundreds of years old. 'Starry columbines', with flat star-shaped flowers, can still be found, and may date from as long ago as the 1500s. *A. vulgaris* 'Nora Barlow' is of the same period. Many forms of this species have naturalized in North America, probably taken there by early colonists.

American gardeners of the seventeenth century were already fond of native species like *Aquilegia canadensis* and *A. caerulea*. John Tradescant had collected and was growing the glowing golden-scarlet *A. canadensis* by 1640. It was to remain popular; Thomas Jefferson grew it at Monticello, where it can still be seen.

All species and varieties of aquilegia are excellent in cottage borders, easily grown, full of colour, and self-sowing and crossing with abandon; they're especially good among irises and oriental poppies, though you could add species asters to give some late summer colour.

Bellis DAISY

There are fifteen species growing in Europe and North Africa. Forms of the common daisy (*Bellis perennis*) are strewn over missals and books of hours of the medieval period. By the late 1500s, fully double flowers in red or white, or with the two colours mixed, were popular and can still be found. *B. perennis* 'Alba Plena' is one, its double daisies packed with petals in purest white.

Other antique varieties still around include: 'Alice' and 'Dresden China' (perhaps eighteenth century); 'Rob Roy' and 'Robert' (nineteenth); and 'Aucubifolia', with leaves flecked with yellow (mid-1800s). Several sorts were grown in America by 1866, when *The American Gardener's Assistant* lists various types, including 'Hen and Chickens', as greenhouse flowers. Seed strains are Victorian or later, fine for the loudest parterres. In cottage gardens use them to edge paths and flowerbeds.

Below: Garden pinks prettily marked like this have been grown since the late seventeenth century, when they were set at the sides of borders in spacious gardens and used for posies, mixed with the buds of damask roses.

Dianthus CARNATION,
PINK, SWEET WILLIAM, CHINA PINK

Carnations and the smaller clove gilliflowers (*Dianthus caryophyllus*) appear in medieval illuminations and portraits, where they are commonly double scarlet, with jagged petals and strong blue-grey leaves. Many flowers in sixteenth- and seventeenth-century illustrations resemble the gorgeous 'Fenbow Nutmeg Clove'. Once eighteenth-century florists got to work, endless new groups appeared, including 'piquettes' (white, splashed with colour), 'flakes' (with irregular stripes of colour radiating along the petals) and 'bizarres' (streaked with three or four different colours). For a real antique, grow 'Raby Castle', in salmon pink, with darker flecks.

The basic species of pink (*Dianthus plumarius*) has small white or palest candy pink flowers, five fringed petals and a delicious clove-like smell. Doubles of these types were popular medieval flowers, and 'Old Fringed White' and 'Old Fringed Pink' are still to be found. Try also 'Caesar's Mantle', which may be from this period.

Feathered or 'starre' pinks known in Britain in the seventeenth century had larger flowers, with frilled petals and often a darkish pink 'eye'. Many, like 'Ragamuffin' and 'Cedric's Oldest', have survived in old gardens. A double form worth having is the deliciously scented 'pheasant's eye'.

In the eighteenth century pheasant's eye types seem to have given rise to fully 'laced' pinks, with red purple edging to the white petal. The finest – 'Dad's Favourite', 'Paisley Gem' and 'William Brownhill' – may be early nineteenth century.

No *Dianthus* species likes being shaded by other plants, so keep them with border auriculas, low-growing thymes and double daisies such as the pale pink 'Dresden China'. For vertical emphasis, add clumps of blue-grey leafed bearded iris.

Sweet Williams (*Dianthus barbatus*) have been in cultivation in several forms at least since the early sixteenth century, and are still vastly popular. A scarlet double was in cultivation by 1634; today's *D. barbatus* 'King Willie' may be a descendant. Single sweet Williams make good edging plants for a grass path through the vegetables.

Above left: The double aquilegia 'Nora Barlow' – a modern name on an ancient plant – makes an excellent border flower, either grown from seed or bought as a mature plant. Keep it away from other aquilegias to ensure that it seeds 'true'.

Above right: Double daisies, flowering in earliest summer, give colour right at the front of the border; in cold regions overwinter them in pots indoors, where they will flower in early spring.

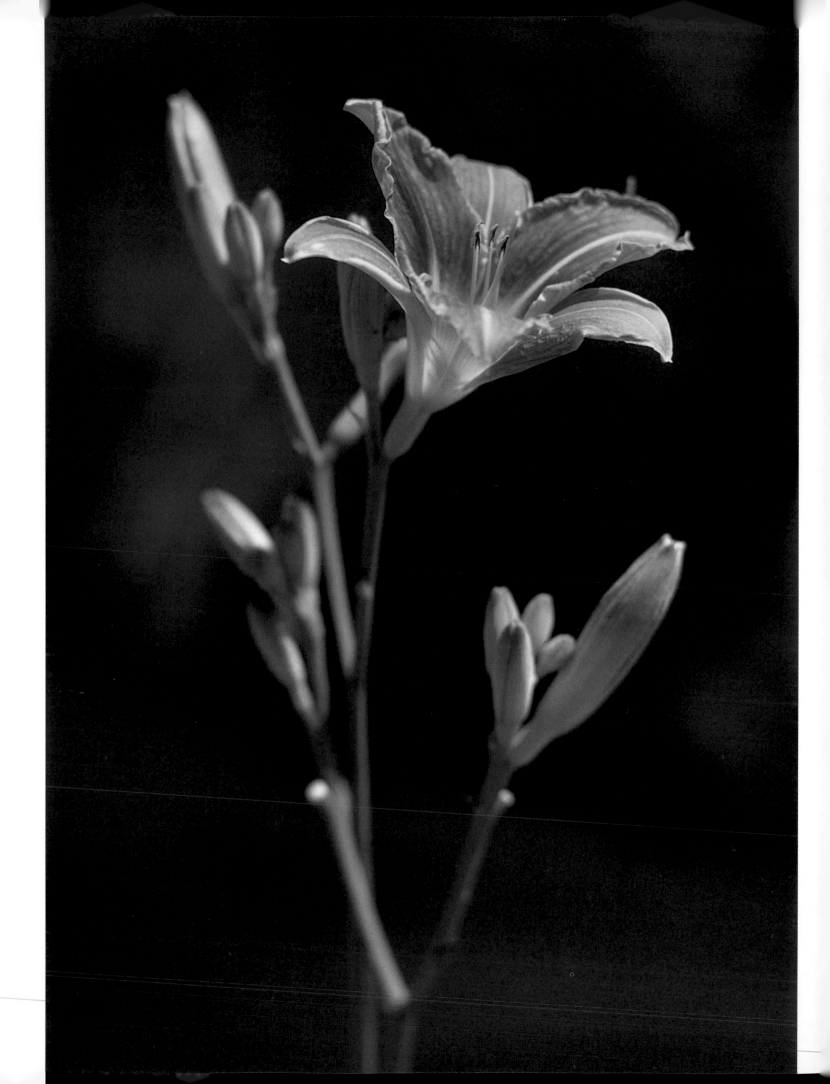

Helleborus CHRISTMAS ROSE, HELLEBORE

There are twenty species of hellebore in cultivation in Europe and Asia, though some are rare. The oldest garden species are *Helleborus niger* (the Christmas rose) and *H. foetidus* (the stinking hellebore), native in all Western European woodlands. Though it may have had medicinal uses, the hellebore was a greatly admired garden plant in the seventeenth century, but seems to have dropped out of use until the late nineteenth.

Helleborus niger, on the other hand, has been used by mankind since neolithic times, and probably as a garden plant since Roman ones. Prehistoric burials sometimes contain seed and capsules, but it may have been used as an arrow poison (it was still used as such by the Gauls) or for religious, medical or magic purposes. The plant was a cure for madness, melancholy and hypochondria well into the seventeenth century, and was planted by cottage doors as a protection from spells into modern times. The seventeenth-century garden writer John Parkinson thought that the 'flowers have the most beautiful aspect, and the time of his flowering most rare, that is, in the deeps of Winter about Christmas, when no other can be seen upon the ground.' They all like shade, so plant them with other shade lovers such as sweet violets and pulmonarias, and add contrasting foliage from *Sanguinaria*.

Hemerocallis DAYLILY

Of the twenty species of daylily from Asia, only two are antique garden plants. One is heavily perfumed and was once called 'yellow tuberose'; the other is an ancient Chinese garden and culinary plant called 'the flower of forgetfulness'. The first is *Hemerocallis lilioasphodelus*, which reached Europe in Roman times and America in the eighteenth century. Flowering early in the

season and with narrow, floppy foliage, it makes a good plant beside garden steps or by a scating area. It is also grown in pots for the conservatory.

The other species is *H. fulva*. The first form may have reached Europe in the 1400s and had brown-red flowers, though ones with red throats and one in pure yellow began to appear in the seventeenth century. The old form is now called 'Europa'. Doubles and bicoloured flowers are all late nineteenth century, though 'Kwanso' types are old orientals. Several sorts were common in American gardens by 1890, and both there and in Europe daylily breeding began in the 1890s. Try pale yellow ones with bloodroots, ferns and aquilegias, with peonies behind.

Above: *Helleborus niger*, the Christmas rose, has probably been a garden plant since Roman times, but seeds and capsules have been found in neolithic burial places.

Opposite: The herbalist John Gerard grew the 'orange tawney' daylily in the early seventeenth century. Now found as *Hemerocallis* 'Europa', it is a vigorous plant, good by steps and doorways.

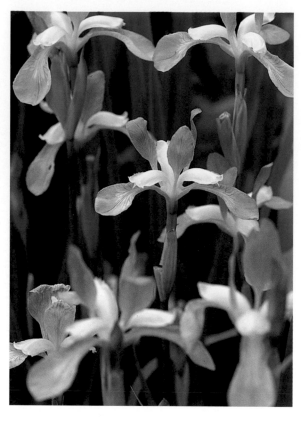

Above left: The sixteenth-century flag iris *Iris foetidissima*, with strange greeny brown flowers, produces magnificent seedpods in late autumn. A form with variegated leaves was popular in the eighteenth century and is well worth seeking out.

Above right: *Iris sibirica* relishes a damp place in the garden and has been a connoisseurs' plant for many centuries.

Iris IRIS, FLEUR DE LUCE

This is one of the great garden genera, with nearly two hundred species in Europe, Asia and through-out North America. Several are among the most ancient of all garden plants. *Iris germanica* and *I.* 'Florentina', the German or bearded irises, are probably the oldest. The first is in shades of blue, the second is silvery white and earlier flowering. As it flowers earlier than many irises, it combines with late tulips; I've often grown it among black parrot tulips, though a softer planting with yellow 'cottage' tulips looks even better. Most other bearded irises date from after 1600, by which time gardens had a number of species. Nowadays, large numbers of bearded irises appear each year, making it a modern florists' group. However, irises have been bred since the 1880s, so antique ones can still be found.

Iris foetidissima has been grown in Europe since the sixteenth century, mostly for its splendid seed capsules, stuffed with orange-scarlet seeds. Try the variegated form in front of euphorbias, as foliage contrast in a drift of pale celandines.

Other suitable species for antique gardens are *I. sibirica* (sixteenth century, though the named forms are modern), *I. xiphioides*, the 'English iris', and *I. xiphium*, the 'Spanish iris', all popular in the sixteenth and seventeenth centuries. The oriental garden species like *I. kaempferi* and *I. tectorum*, though ancient there, have been in European gardens only since the nineteenth century. The enchanting bulbous irises are also, alas, moderns.

All the larger iris species are as valuable for their foliage as their flowers, making good structural accents amid the often hazy planting of cottage flowers. Try them with herbaceous peonies.

Lilium LILY, MARTAGON

In a genus with seventy or so species growing throughout the northern hemisphere, two are among the oldest of domesticated plants, though they were first cultivated because their bulbs are edible: the bulbs are steamed before eating. They are the Madonna lily (*Lilium candidum*) from Anatolia, and *L. tigrinum* from the Far East.

In European gardens, the Madonna lily reigned alone until the early sixteenth century, though she did have several variant forms, including a now rare double. One or two American lilies attempted to usurp her in the 1580s, and a few more in the eighteenth century, including *Lilium philadelphicum* and *L. superbum*.

Other essential cottage lilies include *Lilium martagon,* usually in mauve or purple, though the lovely white form was admired by 1634; and *L. chalcedonicum*, a sumptuous Turkish variety probably first grown by John Gerard from roots imported from Constantinople. Victorian flower arrangers combined it with the Madonna lily and black helleborine (*Veratrum nigrum*), and American gardeners had it by 1740. Try, too, *L. bulbiferum*, which has flowers ringed in orange and cerise, but is tricky to grow. *L. pomponium*, a grand European, is also worth trying; John Rea boasted in the 1660s that his plants had eighty to a hundred flowers on each spike. However, nothing could be easier than a planting of ordinary martagon lilies among drifts of self-sown valerian, tangled with wild strawberries and ferns.

The first Asian lily (*L. dauricum* or *L. pensylvanicum)* arrived in the 1700s, a harbinger of a flood of Japanese, Chinese and Korean lilies that appeared in the West in the nineteenth century.

Above left: This gorgeous spotted leopard lily (*Lilium pardalinum*) from California had been known in America for a century or more before it arrived in European gardens in 1875.

Above right: The Madonna lily (*Lilium candidum*) reached America in 1630. Happy in shade or sun, she is essential in every cottage garden. Try her with veratrums or ferns, all good against a dark background, perhaps an ivy-covered wall or tall hedge.

Paeonia PEONY

An Asian genus, with two American species and a few Europeans. Both the European species and several oriental ones have been grown since gardens began. Furthermore, the gardeners of both continents have been envious of each other, so oriental peonies reached Europe in the early nineteenth century and caused a furore.

Paeonia officinalis, the 'Female peionie', was single in ancient gardens; the lovely double 'peony rose' was in every connoisseur's garden by the seventeenth century and by the end of that century pink and white doubles, packed with petals and smelling just like the flowers of *Rosa gallica*, were available. Plant them in cottage borders, either by themselves or with pulmonarias, honesty, polyanthus and lily of the valley. All of these flowers were cultivated in Puritan America in the 1620s.

Chinese gardeners were compiling lists of tree peony, or moutan, varieties by 700AD. The first reached Europe in the 1790s. The plants are long-lived and old varieties may yet be discovered. European collectors are once again searching Chinese gardens for ancient flowers.

The Chinese herbaceous peony (*Paeonia lactiflora*) was established in Europe only around 1800, but had many varieties in China by 1100AD, and a sixteenth-century nursery stocked thirty. In Europe they were crossed with *P. officinalis* and by the 1850s there were endless gorgeous flowers. Surviving are 'Duchesse de Nemours' (1856) and 'Festive Maxima' (1851), both double whites; 'Marie Crousse' (1892) and 'Baroness Schroeder' (1889), both blush pinks; and 'Madame Calot', deep pink (1856). All flourish in shade: I grow them beneath gnarled apple trees, with veratrums, blue aquilegias and a carpet of *Omphalodes verna*.

Papaver POPPY

A genus of around 100 species found throughout the northern hemisphere, from ephemeral annuals to the flamboyant magnificence of the huge and perennial oriental poppy (*Papaver orientale*).

The Iceland poppy (*Papaver nudicaule*) was introduced in the early 1700s and the miniature *P. alpinum*, a close relative of the more recent *P. burseri*, a few decades later. *P. orientale* seems to have been in some European gardens by the 1600s and a common garden plant by the 1700s. Grow the single scarlet one among campanulas and artemisias, and all the forms of opium poppy (*P. somniferum*) you can find. The basic species has single flowers in white or a dingy mauve, but even some of the brightly coloured sorts may be 3,000 years old. The double white was grown in New England in the seventeenth century, and many garden varieties are mentioned in the 1700s, among them a double black (still obtainable) and a 'double jagged Poppy, with beautiful striped flowers' (probably vanished).

If you want to use opium poppies in the garden, try a planting from Moorish gardens of the 1300s, especially admired for viewing by moonlight: grow them beneath medlars, pears, plums, cherries and peaches, all twined with jasmine, and among the fresh green foliage of lupins, the lush glossy leaves of mandrake, white lily and mint.

The oriental poppy does not seem to have been described as a garden plant much before 1714. The brilliant scarlet and black-purple centred one was the only variety cultivated until the early 1800s, when several closely related species arrived, including *Papaver bracteatum*, from the Caucasus and Persia in 1817; *P. pilosum,* from Asia Minor in 1852; *P. rupifragum* from Spain and *P. atlanticum* from Morocco in 1889. These were crossed to give some of the exciting varieties listed today. Popular sorts from the 1870s include the charming 'Nana Flore Pleno'. Many others, like the white and purple 'Perry's White', are from the early 1900s.

A famous flower arranger of the 1860s, Miss Frances J. Hope, used crimson oriental poppies with straw and dark blue flowered irises, and mixed them with wild Aaron's rod (*Verbascum thapsus*), a combination that would also make a fine antique flower border.

Opposite. The double form of *Paeonia officinalis* (above) has been a garden plant since ancient times; the hybrid 'Sarah Bernhardt' (below) is from 1906 but is related to ancient garden flowers.

Centre: Shirley poppies, bred around 1880, are selections from exotic forms of the wild field poppy (*Papaver rhoeas*), which has been in gardens since at least 1629.

Above: The opium poppy (*Papaver somniferum*), originally cultivated for its deliciously flavoured seed, as well as for the latex obtained from the immature seed capsules – the drug opium.

Primula PRIMROSE, COWSLIP, OXLIP, AURICULA

This is another group that occurs throughout the northern hemisphere, with around 250 species, some much admired in the cottage garden. The primrose, one of the first flowers of spring, is painted in medieval manuscripts, and by the late 1500s dozens of variants were grown. The lovely, and now rare, double was the most valued by 1500. The double white, once again easily available, is also of the early sixteenth century.

The seventeenth century saw ever stranger variants: hose-in-hose (with one flower inside another) and jack-in-the-green (whose sepals are enlarged to make a pretty green ruff). A number of similar types are still available.

Doubles remained popular; *Primula vulgaris* 'Lilacina Plena' (or *P.* 'Quaker's Bonnet'), easy to find and grow, is from the early 1700s, and the slightly darker 'Marie Crousse', pink-violet edged with white, is from the early 1800s: it received an Award of Merit from the Royal Horticultural Society in 1882. All like shade later in summer, so they are good along the path through the gooseberry patch.

The cowslip (*Primula veris*) has a garden history as old as the primrose. There were doubles by the time of John Gerard, whose famous *Herball* was published in 1597, and they continue to be mentioned throughout the eighteenth and nineteenth centuries. Some are still around, if rare.

The polyanthus is a complicated hybrid of *Primula vulgaris* (the word 'polyanthus' was first used in 1683). A specimen was sent from Oxford to Leiden in that year, and in Europe it was called the English primula. Exciting variations soon appeared, and even in the seventeenth century the beginnings of the 'gold-laced' polyanthus were found. They were the deepest red, with a narrow yellow band along each petal. By 1780, John Abercromby, a Scots gardener, wrote that they were 'one of the most noted prize flowers among florists'. Seed arrived in America soon after, and the height of their popularity was reached around 1840, after which there was a rapid decline. Good seed strains can readily be found. Try them beneath roses or by the path, where you can easily examine (or pick) the flowers. They look especially good planted among clumps of daylilies.

Garden auriculas are offspring of *Primula auricula* and *P. hirsuta*. By the end of the sixteenth century, gardeners had hybrids in white, red, yellow and purple. Soon, there were sorts with a thick leaf surface of white wax (which gardeners called 'meal'), some with a similar white 'paste' in the centres of the flowers, and one with the beginnings of striping. Most seventeenth-century auriculas were grown in the open ground, and were similar to modern border auriculas; the fancier varieties were grown in pots, even then. In the eighteenth century, the pots were displayed on 'stages' (rows of shelves covered with an awning over the top to protect the precious 'meal' on leaves and flowers). By then, too, green-edged auriculas were first illustrated.

Border auriculas are easy to grow if they can be given moist, temperate summers with some shade, and even the show varieties are not difficult. However, show auriculas have flowers with 'meal' on them, and this is easily damaged by wind and rain, so they need to be in a cold greenhouse or a special shelter. They grow well in any loam-based compost. Watch carefully for root pests.

Border auriculas, with their subtle colours, shouldn't have to compete with other spring flowers. Give them space to themselves, then plant annuals such as greeny-yellow mignonette and blue cornflowers among them. The auriculas will appreciate the summer shading.

Opposite: The modern green, grey and white-edged auricula cultivars look like the antiques. They are still plants for show, not the open border.

Above: A typical colour of a seed-raised border auricula, velvety and deep.

Below: A gold-laced polyanthus of a form that began to appear in the mid-seventeenth century. In good show forms, the lacing in the middle of each petal should reach to the flower's centre.

Ranunculus RANUNCULUS, BACHELOR'S BUTTONS, FAIR MAIDS OF KENT, BUTTERCUP

The genus has about 300 species, originating from Europe, the Near East and North America. The showiest antique ranunculus, popular from the seventeenth century to the present day, is the half-hardy *Ranunculus asiaticus*. The first plants arrived in Europe in the late sixteenth century, some of them certainly from Syria. For modern antique gardens, most bulb firms list mixes of the 'Turban' sorts popular in seventeenth-century gardens. They're extremely fine, and are in flower with late varieties of tulip.

Among the hardy species, the most attractive, dating from the 1500s, is the double form of the white-flowered *Ranunculus aconitifolius*, called 'Fair Maids of Kent' or 'Fair Maids of France'. This was common in eighteenth-century American gardens. Try it beneath *Syringa × persica*, and with camassias and some of the species gladioli.

Tulipa TULIP

This is one of the great garden genera, with around fifty species originating from the Middle East. While some were known in Italy by the twelfth century, the first real garden tulips, produced by crossing between several species, were grown in Turkey in the early 1500s.

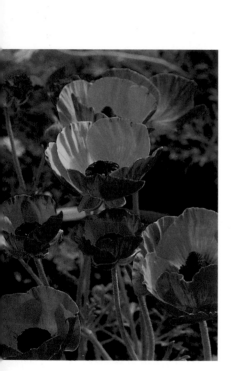

Above: *Ranunculus asiaticus,* an ancient inhabitant of Middle Eastern gardens has become a showy feature of Western ones in early summer.

The first tulip to reach Western Europe flowered in Augsburg in 1559, and was illustrated the next year. Even though it was of a plain colour, it caused a storm of interest. The striped sorts – whose coloration was due to a virus – soon followed, causing even more of a furore. The mania for grand variants was so strong that, in Holland in the next century, a 'futures' market sprang up, with bidders paying colossal sums for bulbs they'd never seen, and would sell on before they had a chance to grow them. In the 1630s, one bulb of 'Semper Augustus' (a variety which lasted into the eighteenth century) was sold for nearly 5,000 florins plus a new carriage and pair.

Valuable tulips were often grown in beds protected by plumed canopies, where their flowers lasted two weeks longer. Societies formed for the breeding and showing of new sorts, though the vogue moved down the social scale, until tulip growing became the preserve of the artisan florists; the Wakefield Tulip Society, described as 'old' in a magazine of 1840, still holds a show every year, with beautifully striped tulips displayed in beer bottles. The varieties shown there, being diseased, are not available in commerce (the kinds described in catalogues as 'Rembrandts' are genetically broken 'Darwins', and are free of infection).

Non-virused sorts were also popular; *Tulipa* 'Keizerskroon' (1750) makes a cheery patch in the cottage borders, and the gorgeous *T.* 'Couleur Cardinal' (1840) is marvellous densely planted in large tubs; it offers one of the most sumptuous reds of any flower. The 'cottage' tulips, so called because many were found in cottage gardens in the late nineteenth century, are probably much

older. 'Mrs Moon' and 'Mothers Day' are favourites of mine; they are happy planted as clumps in the flower border and do not need lifting each autumn. Black parrots, a seventeenth-century type, look splendid among brilliant orange and scarlet ranunculus; or try the sixteenth-century 'Lady Tulip' (*Tulipa clusiana*) among young fern fronds and sedges around a small formal pool. A 'tall yellow' form was popular in nineteenth-century American cottage gardens, and something similar would be good with green-flowered hellebores and palest yellow and white wallflowers.

Above left: A handsome mix of parrot and modern 'Rembrandt' tulips, without the virus that made old 'broken' sorts so lovely. Here, oriental poppies will soon take over the brilliant show.

Above right: The strange, narrow-petalled *Tulipa acuminata* is probably close to early Turkish types.

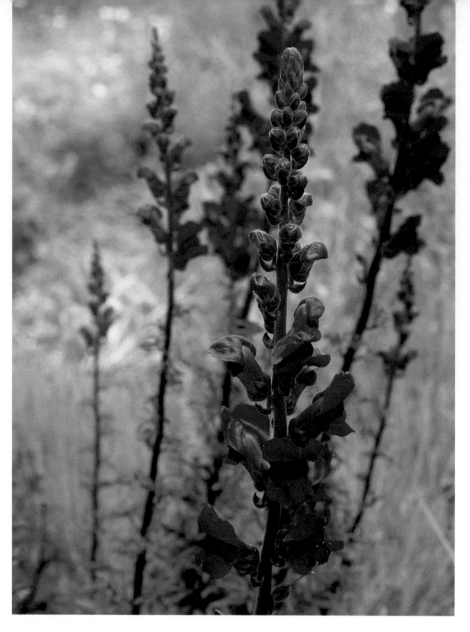

ANNUALS

Above: Snapdragons grow easily from seed, but take autumn cuttings of the best to increase your stock.

Opposite above: 'Art Shades' marigolds, one of the finest antique doubles.

Opposite below: *Cheiranthus* 'Harpur Crewe is ideal for small gardens, growing no higher than 30cm (12in).

Most annuals and biennials are easy to use, and are essential in the modern style of cottage gardening, where they are allowed to self-sow, with the hoe removing only the worst placed of plants. Many cottagers, particularly in the nineteenth century, used them in a piece of eye-catching spring and summer bedding. This was often in the front garden, to give a flourish of colour and show to their houses, with perhaps a diamond-shaped bed or an arrangement of four hearts in a circle, cut into the grass or outlined in glazed tiles. However you want to grow them, the group has lots of delectable antiques.

Antirrhinum SNAPDRAGON

The species most used in bedding is *Antirrhinum majus*, a European native which seems not to have been planted in medieval gardens, but was certainly widespread in sixteenth-century ones; perhaps it had no medicinal use to interest early writers. Wild populations are very variable, and new forms reached the garden slowly over the next two centuries; various of these have been lost, including some with prettily striped flowers. In the eighteenth century there were many named forms, propagated annually by cuttings. Although many were also grown in America, all copy Thomas Jefferson, who had red singles growing at Monticello. For antique gardens, grow tall sorts from seed, in white, rose, red or yellow; white ones, with blue cornflowers, can look splendid between bushes of the rose 'Maiden's Blush'. Well-grown plants can look good in pots, too.

Calendula officinalis MARIGOLD

Calendula is a quintessential cottage flower and so ancient that it has lost any contact with a wild species. It was common in medieval gardens all over Europe, and also known as 'Mary Gowle's', 'Goldes' or 'Ruddes'. At that time marigolds were used in the kitchen (to colour soup and butter and to dilute saffron) and in the medicinal garden (its cordial cured depression). The plants were important enough to arrive in America with the first white settlers.

Doubles were popular by the late 1500s and come now from every seed packet. The strange little hen-and-chicken sort, with florets hanging off the main flower, is also still seen. Plants of the strain known as 'Art Shades' look good among parsley and mint, though in the flower border try them with garnet-red violas and a feathery annual grass such as *Stipa pennata*.

Cheiranthus WALLFLOWER

Though there are American species, the garden wallflower (*Cheiranthus cheiri*) is a plant of the Eastern Mediterranean. The Romans must have brought it to Western Europe, for it was in France and England by 1000AD. No doubt because of sentiment (it has been symbolic of faithfulness in adversity since the fourteenth century) and its lovely smell, it reached America with the first settlers, though young plants must have had winter protection in much of the country.

Singles in brown and yellow (and both) were popular in sixteenth-century gardens, as were white, scarlet and black in eighteenth-century ones. All can still be found, with modern names:

one, 'White Dame', is a fine greenish white. Doubles were in connoisseurs' gardens by the 1580s and were widely used in nineteenth-century ones. Two good doubles, propagated by cuttings, are still available from nurseries: *Cheiranthus* 'Old Bloody Warrior', rich brown, large flowered and heavily perfumed, may be sixteenth century; and *C.* 'Harpur Crewe' is a nineteenth-century name for a double form that would have been familiar to all seventeenth-century gardeners. It is covered in early summer with strongly perfumed flowers. Both make small bushes and look perfect with some of the decorative sages, among irises and beneath cistuses. Nineteenth-century Americans apparently also grew them in the conservatory.

Above: *Lupinus* 'Noble Maiden' is a modern plant based on a number of species that began to arrive in gardens in the early nineteenth century.

Opposite: *Lathyrus grandiflorus* is a splendid scrambling and perennial sweet pea. It is rather invasive, but the flowers have a sumptuous smell: perfect over a fence by the garden gate.

Lathyrus odorata SWEET PEA

Among over a hundred species, this is the most heavily perfumed. In 1699, a Sicilian monk sent seeds to a British gardener, living in Enfield near London. Next season, the London garden was filled with the perfume of the reddish-blue and purple flowers and a garden story began. Although something similar can be found in medieval paintings, it was only now that gardeners became interested. Seed was sold commercially by 1724, and soon new sorts began to appear, including the pink and white variety called 'Painted Lady', still essential in the cottage garden.

Several other old types are still around. 'Lord Nelson' is early nineteenth century and close to the original species. All are vigorous and perfect for growing in traditional ways: twining up obelisks or trellis, or around the kitchen door. Grown thus, they were basic ingredients in American cottage gardens. It is also possible to plant seedlings in the open border and let the plants scramble over rose bushes (try 'Lord Nelson' through Rosa 'Madame Hardy') and up hollyhocks. If you can still reach them, dead-head until late summer, then let pods ripen next season's seed.

Giant or 'Grandiflora' sweet peas date from 1877, but the modern frilled 'Spencers' are all products of the twentieth century.

Lupinus LUPIN

Though there are three hundred species, almost all American, and though they are thought of as conventional inhabitants of cottage gardens, the large, colourful and grandly scented lupins are all modern. However, some of the plain blue or purple seedlings are reasonably close to one of their parents, *Lupinus polyphyllus*, which arrived in Europe from North America in 1826. Breeding began in the 1880s, though bicoloured sorts date only from the 1920s. Antique gardens in Europe can grow the tree lupin (*L. arboreus*), introduced in the eighteenth century, which has yellow, sometimes white flowers; the more graceful *L. perenne*, brought back by Tradescant the Younger from America in 1637; and the ancient annual *L. albus*, which was grown by the Romans for seed oil and admired for its scent. American gardeners do not seem to have grown any sorts until the late nineteenth century.

Tree lupins make floppy mounds of foliage rather than anything resembling a tree, so can look good on the margins of a meadow. In the cottage garden, architectural plants make a good contrast: try the immense dark green leaves of acanthus or the elegant linear ones of irises.

All lupins make excellent meadow plants and, being members of the pea family, their roots will add nitrogen to your grassland.

Above left: Pink-flowered sorts of the tobacco plant (*Nicotiana tabacum*) were once popular as balcony plants in summer, though they look as good in big drifts in the cottage border.

Above right: Plain orange forms of *Tropaeolum majus* have been garden plants since the seventeenth century and for sheer garden impact have hardly been surpassed.

Opposite: The late nineteenth-century *Viola* 'Irish Molly' needs careful propagation by cuttings in early spring to keep it going, but the colour makes it worth almost any trouble.

Nicotiana TOBACCO PLANT

A large genus from Central America, containing some good shrubby species as well as the familiar herbaceous and annual sorts. The tobacco plant was among the first imports into England from the West Indies in the fifteenth century, but, though handsome and by the late 1500s available in several varieties, it was not often used in decorative gardens. Over the next two centuries it gained popularity as a way of covering less powerful – and less pleasant – urban smells.

In the nineteenth century, *Nicotiana affinis* and *N. sylvestris* appeared from the Americas, and were first grown in France. The former is best in its white form, looking delightful with Japanese anemones and tall blue salvias. The perfume can fill the garden in late summer evenings. The even more elegant *N. sylvestris* was often used massed in large tubs, though it mixes well in shaded cottage borders, perhaps with peonies and ferns beneath apple trees. The scent is also delicious.

Tropaeolum NASTURTIUM

Of the numerous South American species of *Tropaeolum* (both annuals and perennials), the oldest garden plant is *T. minus*, introduced to Spain in the early sixteenth century. It is still represented by the late eighteenth-century double, 'Hermine Grashoff'. The species that tumbles across the paths of the *grande allée* in Monet's garden at Giverny is *T. majus*, of the late seventeenth century.

Tropaeolum peregrinum is mid-eighteenth century, and *T. speciosum*, the flame flower from Chile, arrived in Europe in 1846. If you have evergreen hedges, put *T. speciosum* at their base.

Viola VIOLET, VIOLA, PANSY

Though we think of this as a quintessential nineteenth-century 'bedding' group, the sweet violet (*Viola odorata*) had been cherished for centuries. Many named sorts date only from the late 1800s, though the 'Czar' is from 1863 – it has the largest flower of all violets, in deepest purple. The leaves, especially after frost, are almost as perfumed as the flowers, so plant this variety next to the path. Mix with woodland strawberries for an even more delightful scent.

The classic pansies, violas and violettas are complicated hybrids that first appeared in London around 1820, though they were partly parented from new American introductions. They were crossed, in the 1860s, into a charming species called *Viola cornuta*. The results were called violas. Named sorts are late nineteenth century: try 'Maggie Mott', 'Bullion', 'Pickering Blue' and 'Irish Molly'. 'Violettas' are more recent; antique gardens are best with *Viola cornuta* in white, blue or amethyst. The blue variant makes a fine foil beneath some of the sharper pink roses or covering the woody rhizomes of bearded irises.

CLIMBERS

The cottage porch or a ramshackle arbour, twined with woodbine, roses and strands of jasmine, was part of the idealized picture that the Victorians had of cottage living. Nor was this just sentimentality. Ever since the sixteenth century, cottage gardens have been places for romantic tangles of climbers, disguising unsightly structures, clambering over pergolas or growing up a framework to shade the sitting areas and provide a shady and fragrant green arbour. They add to the pleasures of even the tiniest spaces, without reducing the garden ground needed for cabbages and lavender. The only modern addition to the cottage 'look' is the vogue for twining climbers into fruit trees, though no ancient cottager would have done this; the fruit crop was too important.

Below: *Clematis* 'Jackman's Purple' caused a sensation when it first appeared in the 1850s, but was soon widely thought of as a cottage flower.

Clematis CLEMATIS, OLD MAN'S BEARD

Despite there being 250 species of clematis scattered over the northern hemisphere, of the big-flowered hybrids, the only antique is 'Jackman's Purple', a nineteenth-century cross between various species. Some grand gardeners hated these innovations and went back to old garden sorts, like *Clematis flammula* (sprawly, scented, perfect through eglantine roses) and the range of forms in *C. viticella*. Both are sixteenth century, though the double *C. viticella* is probably eighteenth. *C. alpina* was an occasional garden plant from the 1790s; *C. montana* is more recent (1830s). All look fine around windows and do well on shaded facades or up rustic supports in the flower borders. *C. alpina* flowers just before apple blossom opens, so try some up an old fruit tree.

Hedera helix IVY

Hedera helix was one of the great nineteenth-century plants, draped over every mantel and sofa arch, and every brown photo of 'the dear departed'. It had also been widely grown in the ancient world, where it was sacred to Bacchus. The yellow-berried 'poet's ivy' (*H. helix* 'Poetica') was grown in Roman gardens and was equally popular in the sixteenth century, when it was hung outside taverns as a sign. It can still be grown. In the eighteenth century there were silver forms and a gold variegated one, but nothing else.

The nineteenth century saw a huge number of new forms, 'Irish' being the most popular. By this time ivy had been equated with rustic charm and cosiness, and commonly covered cottages and villa porches. Both Irish ivy and new variegated sorts were popular for Wardian cases (see page 149). Later in the century, it became associated with tombs and churchyards and, like death, went out of fashion. Try ivies as groundcover, around a shady seat, or twined through palings by the gate.

Ipomoea MORNING GLORY

Though this is a large genus containing shrubs and herbaceous plants, it is the sumptuous blue flowers of the climbing annual *Ipomoea purpurea*, and the cerise or white flowers of its relatives, that have been thrilling European gardeners since the late sixteenth century, when seed was brought from America. Thought to be a species of convolvulus, it was still called Indian bindweed in the eighteenth century. Rampant, it needs warm gardens, or glass in cool ones. It is good in pots, twined up a cane wigwam. The only perfumed species is the white, night-flowering *I. alba*, often in seed lists as *Calonyction aculeatum*.

Above left: The flowers of *Ipomoea purpurea* last for only a morning, opening from furled buds, but they are in such abundance that that hardly matters.

Above right: Ivies like these can bring drama and interest to some of the shadiest parts of the garden, as well as turning blank walls into evergreen hedges.

Opposite: *Lonicera caprifolium* has a delicious scent but is prone to blackfly. It makes a perfect cover for an unsightly wall or shed, in sun or part shade; here it is combined with *Clematis montana*, introduced from the Himalayas in the 1830s.

Below: *Jasminum polyanthum*, an ancient garden plant, easy to grow, pest-proof and with a breath-taking perfume.

Jasminum JASMINE, ZAMBAC

Several species, including *Jasminum officinalis*, *J. sambac* (the Arabian jasmine) and *J. grandiflorum*, have made gardeners swoon for many centuries. The wonderful, but not entirely hardy, white Chinese *J. officinalis* was grown in Persian gardens by the third century, when the Parthian rulers had extensive contacts with China. The plant was so admired that it soon became the symbol of Vohuman, the Zoroastrian archangel of good spirits, divine wisdom and woman's loveliness.

Jasmine spread around the Mediterranean region following the expansion of the Arab empire, and was widely planted in Moorish Spain. It can still be found as one of the plants used for Spanish gloriettas (arbours of rose, jasmine or cypress, used for dining). In seventeenth-century India, many gardens were designed for the night alone, and filled with jasmine and the creamy-white flowered tuberose (*Polianthes tuberosa*).

The jasmine probably reached non-Moorish Europe during the Crusades and was certainly widely planted by the 1300s. Good combinations were, by 1650, made in the gardens at the Villa Borghese in Rome, filled with roses, jasmine, tulips, amaranths, carnations, hyacinths and jonquils. Try it. Among the white peacocks of Isola Bella, in Lake Garda in northern Italy, the early eighteenth-century trellis-work was once covered in jasmine, pomegranates and oranges. Even in chilly Scotland, a seventeenth-century gardener suggested that your 'gates should be twined about with jasmines and honeysuckles'. A Boston gardener, Thomas Hancock of Beacon Hill, imported a few plants to the US from an English nursery in 1736.

The only time that jasmine has been out of favour was in the nineteenth century, when one critic wrote that 'the perfume of some flowers may affect breathing or digestion, or may cause dizziness and fainting'. Don't let that worry you. In cold gardens, try the tougher *Jasminum* × *stephanense*. *J. officinalis* has to be in every conservatory, where it is easy to look after.

Lonicera HONEYSUCKLE, WOODBINE

Of the many species of this climber, the European native hedgerow honeysuckle or woodbine (*Lonicera periclymenum*) has been in gardens probably since ancient Greece and certainly since early medieval times. It exists in several strains, two of which date from at least the seventeenth century. 'Early Dutch' was around every doorway and in the 'wilderness'. 'Late Dutch' (or 'Late Red') often flowers well into the fall and grew in the same places. Both are still essential garden plants. The other European native, *Lonicera caprifolium* (the perfoliate honeysuckle), was widely grown for its scent in the sixteenth century.

A TRADITIONAL COTTAGE PLOT

This American garden, right next to a handsome old clapboard house in Maine, is probably on the site of the garden original to the house. It perfectly shows all the main elements of a cottage garden: the unaffected mingling of old and new, the mix of flowers, fruit and vegetables, and the mix amongst the flowers of perennials such as irises and lilies with annual or biennial flowers such as nicotianas and clary, the assemblage put together in delectable abundance.

Right: With its formal planning and enclosure, clipped topiary and softly coloured, fragrant plants, the garden perfectly complements the old house.

Above: The classic cottager's plant *Lilium regale* is a strong presence in the garden. This is the most common form with pure white, heavily scented flowers, and petals backed in brownish burgundy; there is also an entirely white form, *L. regale* 'Album'.

Right: Late afternoon shadows show off the pale tones of lilies, annual cosmos, and the lovely old biennial clary (*Salvia sclarea* var. *turkestanica*). The planting of red astilbes and the climber *Phygelius aequalis* shows how simple colours and a mix of old and new flowers can make good and easy gardens.

Above: *Clematis viticella*, called 'Lady's Bower', is a European native popular as a garden climber since at least the sixteenth century; gardeners could choose between several forms, including a double purple and a single red.

Left: *Nigella damascena*, the aptly named 'love-in-a-mist', is allowed to self-seed around the garden. It can be sown in autumn, or in early or late spring, for a succession of striking blooms throughout the year. The flowers are followed by attractively shaped seedpods.

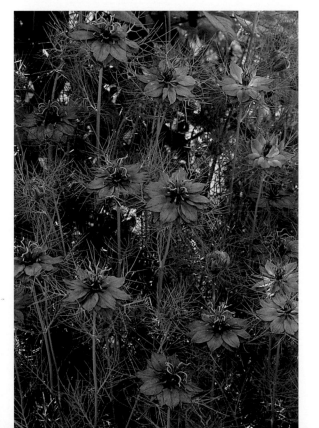

Like all good cottage gardens, too, it is given a strong basic structure, first of all by its enclosure – here handsome, if modern, stone walls neatly palisaded along the top, a perfect place for draping the climbing plants – and secondly by its paths, which make a clear grid of linear brick walkways, as easy to walk on in a wet winter afternoon as on a summer morning.

In this garden, enclosure and paths are combined in a rectangular plan which stops the overflowing planting turning into an out-of-focus mess. Fancifully curved paths may sound 'cottagey', but they end up looking fussy. The strongly linear plan also means that the garden yields visual pleasure even in winter, when all the plants but the topiary evergreens have vanished.

Above left: Remember to position your garden seat so that you benefit from the scent as well as the sight of your plants. In this garden, the dominant perfume is provided by the lilies.

Above right: Veronicas, daylilies and *Eryngium bourgatii*. Veronicas like this were being introduced to gardens from America and Asia in the eighteenth century; the eryngium was in gardens by 1731.

The brick paths here have been laid with great ingenuity, the patterns varying in different parts of the garden to point out the different functions. The kitchen garden part, for instance, has the simplest pattern. The paths are edged with end-up bricks, a useful detail, as they give the margins of the paths more stability when the beds are dug over. Because they suffer severe winters, the owners have used engineering-quality bricks, which don't break up when the dampness in them freezes. However, cottage gardens can have many other possible path surfaces: coarse sand or fine gravel, flagstones or a pattern of different materials.

If you do use bricks, and you want them in herring-bone pattern as in parts of this garden, instead of using expensively cut bricks to straighten off the edges, plant lines of thymes, double daisies or border auriculas and let them disguise the ragged edge. With gravel, box edgings are good, keeping the gravel firmly in its place.

The 'kitchen' section of this garden has dwarf borders made of low espaliers of apples, great fun to look at though tricky to maintain. The main planting of fruit here is in a proper orchard, but if your garden isn't large enough to allow that, then plant a fruit tree or two amongst the flowers, and as the tree grows, use more and more shade-tolerant flowers beneath.

The strongest scent in this highly perfumed garden comes from *Lilium regale*, not quite an antique (1903) but so easy to grow that it has almost eclipsed the other white lily, the much older *L. candidum*. For evening scent, the nicotianas, especially *N. sylvestris*, are unbeatable.

Colours are fairly muted, with a few splashes of brilliance, the most intense provided by the climber on the paling, *Clematis jackmannii* 'Superba', developed by an enterprising plantsman, Mr Jackman, in the 1850s.

The perennial flower planting provides good 'bones' later in the season, with linear-leafed antiques such as *Iris sibirica*, some broader-leafed *I. germanica* hybrids, and daylilies, with the more softly structured nigellas, aquilegias, asters, centaureas, phlox and herbs.

A cottage garden is also defined by its non-plant props: water butts, bird houses, pots and seats. This garden is filled with charming ideas. Though you might not have a lead water cistern like the one pictured here, you can easily copy its enchanting planting in any big container: a mix of a dark purple-blue heliotrope (try 'Gatton Park') and the delightful peppermint-scented and velvety-leafed *Pelargonium tomentosum*. Both were favourites with the Victorians.

The garden also has a rustic seat – a style popular in the late 1800s and the early decades of this century – which looks especially comfortable among plants of the same date: *Salvia argentea*, daylilies and the silvery seedheads of the Chinese *Clematis orientalis*, introduced to Europe much earlier, in 1731. However, almost any sort of seat, if made of a natural material, will be perfectly appropriate, and give you somewhere to relax and enjoy the antique flowers.

Above: A splendid lead tank is filled with heliotrope in deep purple; a few good-sized plants will perfume a whole garden.

Left: A low framework of espaliered apple trees makes a charming foil to the paths. The bricks are laid In patterns that differ throughout the various sections of the garden. In the foreground, bell jars make attractive cloches for young salad plants.

THE WILDFLOWER GARDEN

Throughout its history, garden design has swung between the polarities of deliberate artifice and a hankering for the delights of unembellished nature, or it has sought to accommodate both styles within the same plot. In ancient Rome, for example, gardens commonly had formal flowerbeds and topiary, but they also included areas that were supposed to be the mirrors of true wilderness.

In early medieval gardens, the 'flowery mead' was trim and sophisticated wilderness on a tiny scale, somewhere to sit in the warmth of summer, to flirt, eat, play music or listen to poetry. During times of war and plague, it gave solace, as it did to the inhabitants of Boccaccio's *Decameron*, who fled to where '...in the middle of the garden was a square plot, after the semblance of a Meadow flourishing with high grass, herbs and plants, beside a thousand diversities of flowers, with orange and lemon trees, all around. At the centre a fountain of white carved marble had a gush of water, springing from a statue put on top of a column...'

Left: Meadow flowers, with their immense profusion and often small scale, make gardeners intensely aware of the subtlety of light, often in ways that the more brilliant garden flowers do not allow. Above: Wildflowers of all sorts, from campions and soapworts to bluebells and lords and ladies, show their full beauty in meadow or woodland gardens.

By the time of the Renaissance, the sophisticated flowery mead had gone out of fashion, but many grand gardens had wildernesses instead. Though the earliest example seems to have been built at Hesdin, in northern France, in the fourteenth century, 250 years later every European palace and country house, from Versailles to Hampton Court and Chatsworth, had them, as did small manor houses like Tixall Hall, in rural Derbyshire. The area near the house or palace was given over to topiary, knots and parterres (whose intricate patterns could be appreciated from upstairs windows), and very visible artifice and cost; further away, the wild garden or wilderness (decorated with 'classical' elements such as fountains, pavilions, statuary and arbours) was still very much a place to display wealth and learning – now often of decidedly pagan motifs and ideas – rather than somewhere to copy countryside and forest.

And so, with minor changes, it was to remain all over Europe until the early eighteenth century, when in England the pendulum of taste swung off course in a dramatic way. The landscape movement, with its very idealized vision of the wilderness, suddenly swept away obvious gardens, with their parterres, flowers, statues and topiary. The model for the new style was not, as one might have expected, the wild countryside or farmland of Britain, but the landscape painting of a handful of artists who had lived mostly in Italy during the seventeenth century. It was all very grand, with scythed lawns sweeping up to the walls of the house and the lake kept tidy and glittering. To add to the drama of the view – and to show off – grand temples, often modelled on fragments of Roman ones, and statuary were all carefully placed for the most painterly effect.

All this was fine if the garden owner had vast acreages of spare land, but impossible to emulate for those with less. So, in about 1820, an intense reaction against 'landscape' set in, and one strand of the reaction was a renewed passion for old-fashioned gardens, parterres, topiary and all the artifice of the seventeenth century. It led eventually, amongst civilized if not rich gardeners, to the cottage garden movement. Another strand was an attempt to imitate authentic and picturesque nature without the trim lawns and classical buildings of the landscape garden. Though called 'the picturesque' at the time, amid much heated debate, this movement soon gave rise to the wild garden, which, in the hands of its most publicity-conscious proponent, the magazine-owning William Robinson, made use not only of European wild flowers, but of the species of all other continents too.

The wild garden embraced a rather precious feeling for the untamed nature of forest or half-wild countryside, as well as a nostalgia for the rich flora and wildlife of ancient meadows increasingly being ploughed up by modern farmers using new agricultural techniques and chemicals.

While poets have appreciated wild woodlands since ancient times, conservative gardeners have taken rather longer to see their beauties. The 'wildernesses' described above would, to most modern eyes, have seemed entirely artificial. Even the more modest versions had the paths edged with wild strawberries, clipped ivy, box or even flowers like double primulas, hepaticas or polyanthus.

A closer approximation to real woodland was, sometimes, the 'American garden', a vogue that started in Europe in the closing decades of the eighteenth century, when American tree and shrub species began to be grown in large numbers. Many of these, often of great beauty, had been collected along the rivers, the easiest routes for exploring the continent. All, therefore, liked the same environment – damp, peaty soils – and so the American gardens tried to copy these conditions. Some followed the old wilderness formula, except that the path, under the influence of the landscape movement, went in curves rather than straight lines. On the other hand, many were left more properly wild.

The idea lasted well into the nineteenth century and the flora gradually expanded, until eventually it included rhododendrons from the East and from America, camellias from Japan and so on. The look remained artificial, and only by the close of the nineteenth century were gardeners happy to have a piece of natural woodland, and plant among the shadows the lovely woodland flora from all over the globe.

However, interest in the older forms of 'wilderness' is reviving and can offer an exceptionally attractive, labour-saving and interesting way of gardening. Indeed, the woodland garden, like the sacred groves of ancient Greece, can be among the most satisfying and mysterious types of garden.

Above: Bluebells (*Hyacinthoides non-scriptus*) painted by Beatrice Parsons about 1900. Other antiques, such as dog's-tooth violets, lungworts, lily of the valley, and epimediums, can give equally delectable and perfumed sheets of colour.

Opposite: Canterbury bells (*Campanula medium*), here painted by Redouté, have been a gardener's favourite since medieval times.

THE WILD GARDEN TODAY

Wildflower gardening has moved on since the late nineteenth century, on the one hand becoming 'green' (in the political sense) and even hard-line by insisting on the rigorous use of native species alone. While that idea has some appeal, it seems to deny the fact that plants have always moved to new territories, and that the astonishing speeding up of this process over the last two hundred years must simply be accepted. There is no reason why a 'meadow' in Europe should not have flowers or grasses from the Andes or the Himalayas, or one in Arkansas have plants from Central Asia or New Zealand. Or, more importantly, why a new meadow or woodland should not be scattered with antique flowers, wild or sophisticated, and still cherished, from gardening's own past.

The only shadow over the meadow garden ideal is that meadows, or prairies, were grazed by stock, which is impossible in the decorative meadow. In a way, the artificial medieval concept of the flowery mead is more apposite. Even if it is mown rather than grazed, the meadow can be a delectable place, requiring almost nothing in the way of regular maintenance, yet still be filled with narcissi and scillas in earliest spring, scattered with intense cerise corn flags and milky blue camassias in summer, with the last of the butterflies flittering over autumn crocuses at the end of the season.

Your woodland garden, wilderness or fruitful orchard can be carpeted with wild strawberries, sweet violets and bloodroots, and filled, through almost the entire year, with the perfumes of daphnes, sweet box, musk roses, lilac and honeysuckle, while its paths are edged with snowdrops and wild primulas. What a bounty.

If you're starting a meadow garden from scratch, spare a thought for the grasses which will be the main bulk of the planting. The area in which you live will have large numbers of native grasses and, for the planting to look authentic, as many of them as possible need to be represented. Grass seed mixtures designed for lawns will hold almost none of them, so, if you can, sow a wild grass seed mixture harvested from local meadows.

If you are starting from an already half-wild piece of grassland, establish the flowers as almost mature potted plants, and remove the grass for 30cm (12in) or so around each new plant. If you merely scatter wildflower seed over grassland, almost nothing will germinate.

Right: The harebell (*Campanula rotundifolia*) makes a delightful and vigorous meadow plant. It will prefer to grow in the more frequently mown places.

Opposite: The cornflower (*Centaurea cyanus*) is a good meadow flower in both Europe and America, particularly in the first few seasons: before the grasses get too dense, you can have drifts of its flowers.

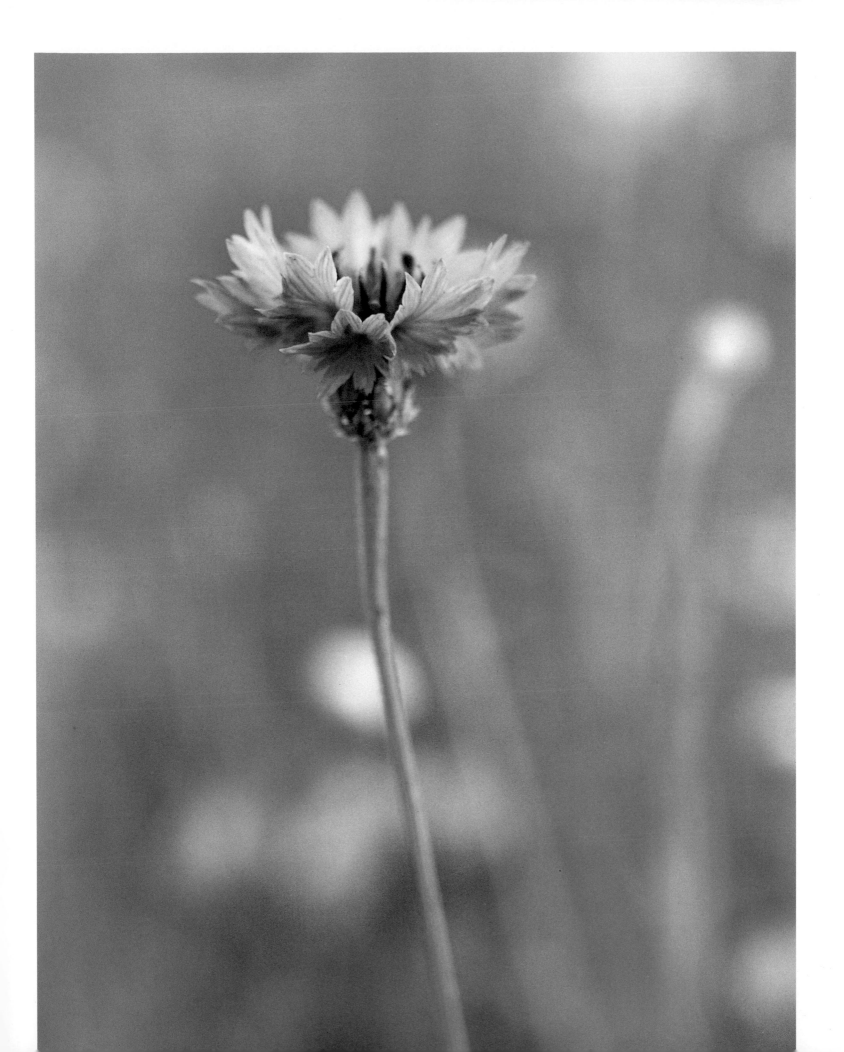

MEADOW BULBS

Many bulbs are natural denizens of meadow and woodland, spending inhospitable seasons below ground. These dormant periods are used to escape drought, or low light levels when the surrounding trees are in full leaf, or cold. Bulbs can enliven your greensward and your grove in earliest spring. Keep the former scattered with summer colour until the first mowing, and brighten autumn in the latter as the branches above begin to scatter their leaves; to see a piece of light autumnal woodland, filled with cyclamen and autumn crocuses, is one of the great excitements of gardening.

The plants don't have to be special: a wood filled with bluebells or the 'Lent Lily' narcissus can be as breathtaking as if it were scattered with rarities. Leave mowing the meadow until most of the bulb foliage has yellowed – for narcissi, that's at least six weeks after flowering; for some alliums, it is only a week or two; and for things like camassias it seems to depend on the season.

All the bulb species below are tolerant of rough-and-ready planting, and it is usually simplest to lift a divot of turf with a spade, nestle a bulb or two into the soil beneath, then replace the turf. Large bulbs such as *Fritillaria imperialis* need to have a hole excavated for them so that the turf can be replaced. Firm the turf down, but not hard enough to damage the bulb.

Though many of the bulbs described here will begin to colonize your meadow in a season or two, plant initially as generously as you can so that in the area devoted to each species you start off with a reasonable show. In all but the tiniest meadow, and with any but the largest of bulbs, any planting of less than 50 per 'patch' will hardly be visible. Keep the patches looking as natural as possible by spacing bulbs closely at the centre, perhaps 30cm (1ft) apart, and scattering them more distantly at the margins.

Camassia CAMASSIA

The five species of camassias, all American in origin, grow easily in moist grassland and have spires of starry flowers, in shades of blue that can vary from deep sapphire to milky pale, or, in some forms of *Camassia leichtlinii*, to palest cream. The bulbs of *C. quamash* were a food crop for Native Americans, though they must also have admired the dark blue flowers. In European gardens from

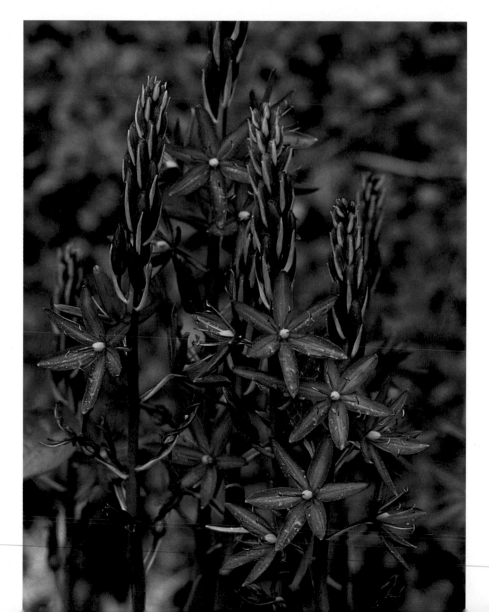

Below: *Camassia leichlinii*, in shades of blue from deep and thrilling to pale and milky, soon makes strong clumps which can be divided every few seasons to stop them getting cramped.

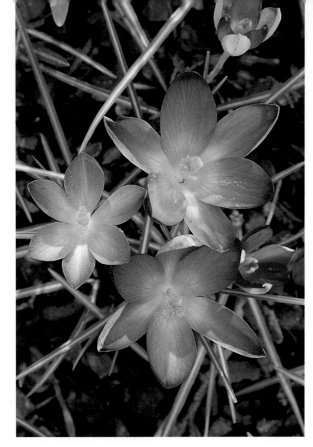

1827, there are several garden forms. Taller and grander, *C. leichtlinii* arrived a few decades later. All its forms are worth having and there's a very special double cream one. All but this variety produce seed; sow it in pots if you need more plants, and keep seedlings potted for a season or two before planting out in the meadow.

Colchicum AUTUMN CROCUS

In spite of their common name, the autumn crocuses are not closely related to autumn-flowering species of the genus *Crocus*. The sixty or so species, all Old World, have fascinated gardeners since Roman times. The one widely grown then, and all over medieval Europe, was the native *Colchicum autumnale*. Singles and doubles in rosy pink, purple and white were once grown and can still be found. At least one form was taken to North America by the first Dutch settlers. All look lovely studding the greensward that grows back in after the last mow of summer.

Grander varieties arrived in the sixteenth century from Constantinople, where they had been popular for many centuries before that. *Colchicum byzantinum* is small-flowered but worth looking at; plant it by a path so that you can see its chequered petals. For meadows in the nineteenth-century style, grow varieties of *C. speciosum*: all have large flowers, and the white one is a marvel. Don't mow until the leaves shrivel away in early summer. Divide the clumps every few seasons or they will stop flowering.

Crocus CROCUS

Saffron, the autumn-flowering *Crocus sativus*, has been grown since the beginnings of civilization and has lost touch with any wild species. It will naturalize in warm and sunny grassland, but is not worth trying in short-summer gardens. Elsewhere, for spring, try the lovely, honey-scented *C. susianus* (syn. *C. angustifolius*, Cloth of Gold crocus), popular since the sixteenth century, or the enchanting *C. imperati*, in favour since the seventeenth. Most other spring crocuses are modern hybrids, though *C. tommasinianus* is just antique and naturalizes easily. For autumn, *C. speciosus* is equally easy and occurs in several varieties, notably 'Artabir' with deep violet-mauve flowers.

Above left: *Colchicum speciosum* 'Album', one of the grandest whites, is a strong grower with large summer leaves. Look for seedpods once the leaves have unfurled: seed takes two winters to germinate.

Above right: *Crocus tommasinianus*, one of the earliest crocuses to flower, makes a dazzling start to the season and will increase well.

Above: Plant the poet's
narcissus by a seat or path
and enjoy the perfume.

Below: *Scilla peruviana*
brings color to summer
meadows, as it did in the
eighteenth century.

Fritillaria FRITILLARY

Though there are some beautiful American species that would do well in a wildflower garden, the most ancient garden fritillarias are European or Near Eastern: *Fritillaria meleagris* (the snakeshead fritillary) and *F. imperialis* (the crown imperial). The snakeshead, with its petals chequered in purple and cream, is an easy meadow plant. Flowering early, it can make a fine, if subtle, show. If you want more impact, plant the white variant, which is also sixteenth century.

The impressive *Fritallaria imperialis* has been grown since the late 1500s. It does best in shade and in warm gardens. Though handsome in flower, it smells powerfully of fox, so do not plant it near the house. The lemon-yellow *F. imperialis* 'Lutea' looks best in meadow grass. Some varieties reached America in the late 1600s and may have been grown by Dutch settlers even earlier.

The black-flowered *Fritillaria persica* and green *F. pyrenaica* have been gardened since the seventeenth century, though only daring gardeners in warm climates will risk them in the meadow. All other species are recent arrivals in the garden.

Narcissus DAFFODIL, NARCISSUS, JONQUIL

This is an extraordinary genus, an assemblage of thirty-five species, but thousands of hybrids. It is filled with antiques, from the 'sacred Chinese lily', one of the tazetta types which reached Europe from ancient Egypt or Greece via China, to the 'Van Sion' daffodil grown by the Tradescants. The easily naturalized Lent lily (*Narcissus pseudo-narcissus*), with its pale yellow twisted perianth lobes and deeper yellow trumpet, has been grown since the sixteenth century.

All the poet's narcissi or pheasant's eye are another group from the ancient world; they are happy in the wild garden and smell delicious. The

largest meadows should have only a handful of varieties, preferably spread through the flowering season. An egg-yellow sort such as 'Van Sion' looks good with pale cowslips, even better with oxlips, and a scattering of fritillaries. The late-flowering 'poet's narcissus' is a perfect partner to the first campions.

Above and left: *Fritillaria meleagris* was used by Elizabethan ladies to decorate their dresses; their Dutch counterparts in New Holland may have done the same. It went on to become a popular cottage garden flower.

Scilla SQUILL

Though antique gardens once sported the pretty flowers of *Scilla bifolia* and *S. peruviana*, the antique most easily established in the meadow garden is *S. sibirica*, which has been popular in European gardens since the eighteenth century. Once established, it seeds very happily and few gardeners can ever have enough of its glorious deep blue flowers at the high point of spring. A white form of *S. peruviana* was much prized in the eighteenth century.

The European bluebell is now placed in another genus (*Hyacinthoides*); it makes an easy and sometimes spectacular meadow plant.

MEADOW ANNUALS AND BIENNIALS

Surprisingly few annuals grow in meadows, where the dense growth of grass makes their lives hard. Poppies, corn marigolds and fumarias are really weeds of disturbed or ploughed soil. Still, try a few. They're best established as part-grown potted plants, and set out in a patch of bare earth. Biennials, too, can make a good show, starting with the purple honesties (keep them well away from the brighter yellow sorts of daffodil, or plant honesties with white flowers) and carrying on into the summer with perfumed drifts of *Hesperis matronalis*. All of them are best planted near tree trunks or the shrubby margins of your meadow.

Hesperis SWEET ROCKET, DAME'S VIOLET

The billowing sprays of white or mauve scented flowers of the biennial *Hesperis matronalis* were much admired in medieval gardens; a double white form appeared in the sixteenth century. This is still around, but tricky to grow and keep over winter; it is something to be cherished in the flower garden, not planted in the meadow. The singles seed happily, so leave the flowering shoots to mature into late summer.

Lunaria HONESTY

Honesty (otherwise known as white sattin flower, balbonac, penny flower, money flower, silver plate, pricke-sangwoort, sattin) was a favourite of medieval gardeners and was even mentioned by Chaucer, who is not usually regarded as a source of garden information.

Now *Lunaria annua* is commonly found in hedgerows and meadow gardens. With a large number of variants within the species, the flowers range from burgundy to white, with lots of reddish purples in between, and the leaves are sometimes dramatically variegated, making the plants look almost too busy. The fleshy roots of *L. annua* were once eaten in salads, perhaps explaining why honesty was one of the first European garden plants to reach America.

Lunaria rediviva, a perennial, had the same uses and is happy in the wild garden, though it prefers more shade. It's a good plant for the difficult area where meadow blends into woodland. The pale violet flowers have a scent that carries well on the spring air. The seedpods, pointed and elliptical, are less good for drying.

Oenothera EVENING PRIMROSE

Most species of *Oenothera* are American, though there is a Tasmanian representative. They have become naturalized in every other continent and can be troublesome weeds. Don't risk them in the flower garden; let them take their chance in the meadow, where their large yellow flowers, often nicely scented, look well. *O. stricta* (sometimes called *O. odorata*) arrived in 1790 and the short and perennial *O. acaulis* was used as a decorative edging plant in Victorian shrubberies and wildernesses. It can be established in the meadow.

Above: Purple or white-flowered *Hesperis matronalis* provides one of the essential scents of a summer afternoon – plant it anywhere you are likely to put a seat

Left: Once seeds and outer casing have been shed, the translucent membranes of honesty's seedpods make good decoration well into winter, and last even longer indoors.

Opposite: Evening primroses are too invasive for cottage borders, so make perfect plants for wild areas and meadows. This is *Oenothera biennis*, which was sent to Padua from Virginia in 1619.

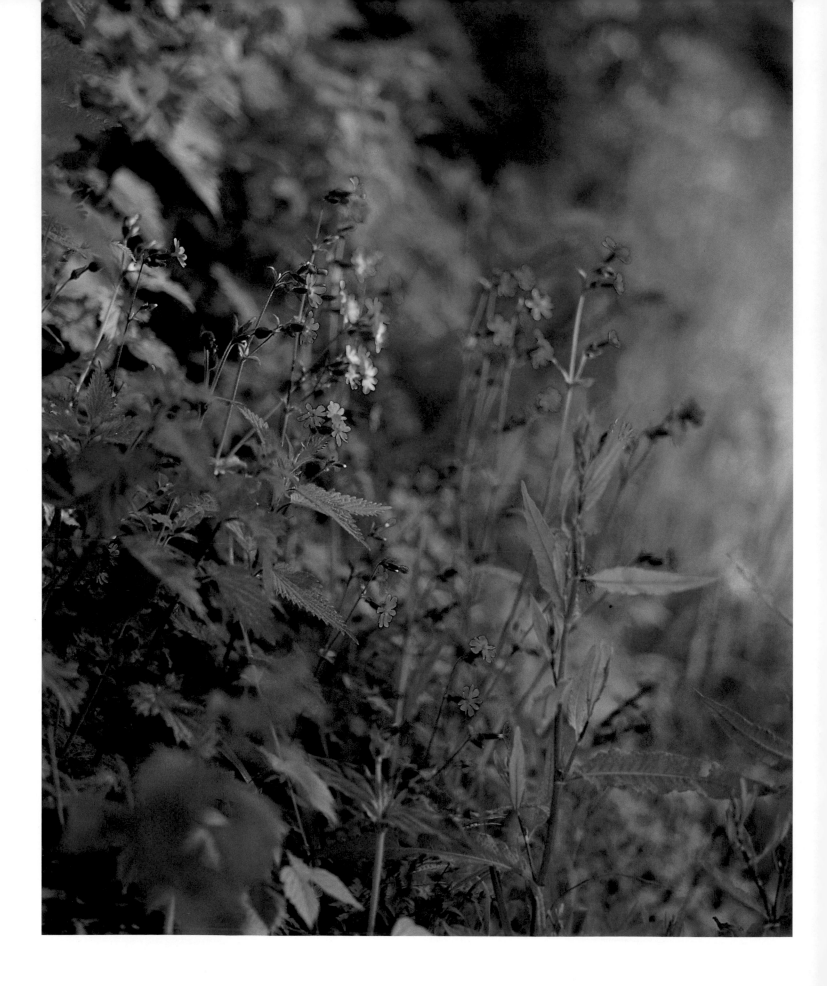

MEADOW PERENNIALS

Though ladies' smock and cowslips will be in flower with the last of the bulbs, most meadow perennials flower in summer. All are best planted in discrete drifts, with initial plants at around 1m (3ft) spacings, with a few more distant 'outliers'. Plant the smaller ones close to mown paths, allowing larger plants to register from further off.

If you are planting directly into established grassland, watch all new plants carefully through-out their first season. Grasses are competitive, and will steal water and light away if they can.

While some tall perennials will tolerate a mow in late summer (plants like *Lythrum salicaria*, *Solidago*, *Echinacea* and *Papaver orientale*), the best ones are low-growing, or have flat rosettes of leaves which remain beneath the mower blades.

Cardamine LADY'S SMOCK
Cardamine pratensis is essential in the meadow, where its four petals shine amid the young grass of late spring. Though it seems to do perfectly well in ordinary grassland, if you have a dampish meadow try the much grander double forms. There are several minor variants, in slightly differ-ent shades of mauve, enchanting, and popular since the mid-1700s. If you want something in white, try *C. trifolia*; gardened since the sixteenth century, it will give you drifts of tiny white flowers where meadow joins shrubbery or wilderness.

Primula PRIMROSE, COWSLIP, OXLIP
Though these also appear in the cottage garden (see page 33), the simpler sorts of primrose (*Primula veris*), cowslip (*P. vulgaris*) and the greeny-yellow oxlip (possibly a hybrid between them, but given the name of *P. elatior*) deserve a place here too. Try the rosy-purple form *P. vulgaris sibthorpii*, especially by a mown path or beside a rustic seat. It is extremely floriferous, an unusual colour so early in the season, and has been grown since the sixteenth century.

Silene CATCHFLY, CAMPION
Many of the catchflies and campions make good meadow plants. Ragged Robin (*Lychnis flos-cuculi*) is especially good, and you can find an amusing white-flowered variant. For perfume, try the closely related soapworts (*Saponaria officinalis*), in marshmallow pink or white, single or double. Mown after flowering in midsummer, the roots will soon make splendid and strong-growing clumps.

Opposite: Red campions make easy meadow plants, grow well on shady banks and look lovely in long grass beneath old apple trees.

Below: Cowslips (*Primula vulgaris*) establish well in dampish meadows; in this one it is grown with the pale lilac *Cardamine pratensis* in its wild single form. The doubles are pretty too, but do best in the cottage garden.

WOODLAND FLOWERS

So much of the garden is designed for sunshine and summer that it is easy to forget that tree species are the natural dominant plant type over much of the land area of our planet. Huge numbers of smaller plants have evolved growing among or beneath them, and have of necessity learned to cope with varying degrees of shade, intense root competition, even drought. In temperate forests, where the trees are mostly deciduous, the subsidiary plants often produce their own foliage and flowers early in the year, before the branches above become thick with leaves.

Among this vast woodland flora are to be found some of the most delectable of all garden flowers, and some of the finest are true antiques in the garden. All gardeners should try to grow at least some of those listed below, and those with shady gardens – whether woodland or urban shade – should plant everything they can find. The rewards, for surprisingly little effort, are enormous.

Aconitum MONKSHOOD, WOLFBANE

The aconitums of evil reputation (their juices were once used to tip poisoned arrows and for baiting a lamb's carcass to destroy wolves) make splendid flowers for light woodland, especially if the soil is damp. They are less spectacular in dry soils. The first into cultivation seems to have been *Aconitum napellus*, its flowers found in medieval manuscripts and a popular garden plant by the Renaissance. Seventeenth-century forms had pink (*A. napellus* 'Carneum') or white (*A. napellus* 'Albidum') flowers. *A. septentrionale*, the yellow wolfsbane, is also medieval, but Victorian wild gardens often combined it with 'gardeners' garters' (the striped-leafed grass *Phalaris arundinacea*) and the droopy white plumes of *Aruncus sylvester*. North America has its own species of aconite (*A. uncinatum*), introduced to Europe in 1770, though the European ones were certainly in American gardens by the nineteenth century.

Right: *Aconitum napellus* should be planted in large clumps for maximum impact and the roots divided every few seasons.

Far right: None of the varieties of *Convallaria majalis* excels the single white form, with its glorious perfume.

Convallaria LILY OF THE VALLEY

Lily of the valley (*Convallaria majalis*), with its tiny white or pink flowers, is an ancient garden plant, since at least 1000BC. Unsurprisingly, there are many variants. Pink- and red-flowered forms were popular in the Renaissance, an inelegant (and still available) double-flowered white was grown by 1770 and ones with leaves variegated in white or yellow appeared a century later (variegations fade as summer progresses). The old white form was a popular cottage garden flower in eighteenth-century North America, but seems to have gone out of fashion in the 1880s. Though they look good by woodland paths, plant a few wherever you have a seat, in sun or shade. Then savour their scent in early summer.

Cyclamen CYCLAMEN, SOWBREAD

The old 'sowbread' is *Cyclamen coum*, first grown probably in Roman times as a medicine for pigs, but as a garden plant since the sixteenth century. Other hardy sorts have been connoisseurs' plants since the seventeenth century, all popular because they flourish in the driest shade beneath shrubs and trees where little else will grow. They make a memorable sight when in sufficient quantity, rendering the shade rose purple in either autumn or spring. They seed happily once you have several corms established.

All were grown in America by 1725, and are popular woodland garden plants there today. In my garden in southern Scotland we grow them with polypody ferns and epimediums.

Above: Cyclamens seed themselves easily once a few plants are established in woodland without much undergrowth. Sheets of them can make astonishing sights in early autumn or spring.

WOODLAND SHRUBS

Above: *Philadelphus coronarius* 'Variegatus', a delightful bush of the eighteenth century, does best in light shade.

Below: The hydrangea-like head of the guelder rose, perfect in spring, goes on to produce translucent scarlet berries.

If the tree canopy is to be provided by native species or standard fruit trees, then below them, or at the margins of the woodland or grove, a shrub layer is essential. If your woodland is composed mostly of native trees, then native shrubs will fit both ecologically and visually. However, the emphasis on the use of native species is quite modern, and certainly before 1860 or so, most gardeners would have planted decorative shrubs that came originally from all over the globe. If you want to use decorative trees too, then great pleasures await you, whether among well-known genera like *Prunus*, *Acer*, *Cornus*, *Magnolia*, *Sorbus*, or from less familiar ones such as *Pterocarya*, *Ailanthus* or *Styrax*.

Euonymus SPINDLE TREE
Euonymus europaeus, the only European of this fascinating genus, most of whose species come from America or Asia, was popular in the wilderness, pruned into a small tree. The red autumn leaves and curious scarlet capsules still make it an exciting plant to grow. By the eighteenth century, *E. americanus* (discovered in 1683) and *E. verrucosus* were becoming popular alternatives. All are unjustly neglected nowadays and should be used much more widely for small shaded gardens, as well as in woodland.

Philadelphus MOCK ORANGE, PHILADELPHUS
Many of the hybrid philadelphuses were bred in the late nineteenth century, as Chinese and North American species began to arrive in Europe in quantity. Only the European *Philadelphus coronarius*, as splendidly perfumed as any of them, is an old garden plant. It is one of the great smells of summer, enjoys woodland conditions and can be left to its own devices. If you want more excitement than the basic species offers, look for the splendid variegated form of the 1770s.

Skimmia SKIMMIA
Early nineteenth-century urban gardeners throughout industrialized Europe were always desperate for plants that would survive the intense air pollution, that were preferably evergreen and had brilliant berries. *Skimmia japonica*, introduced in

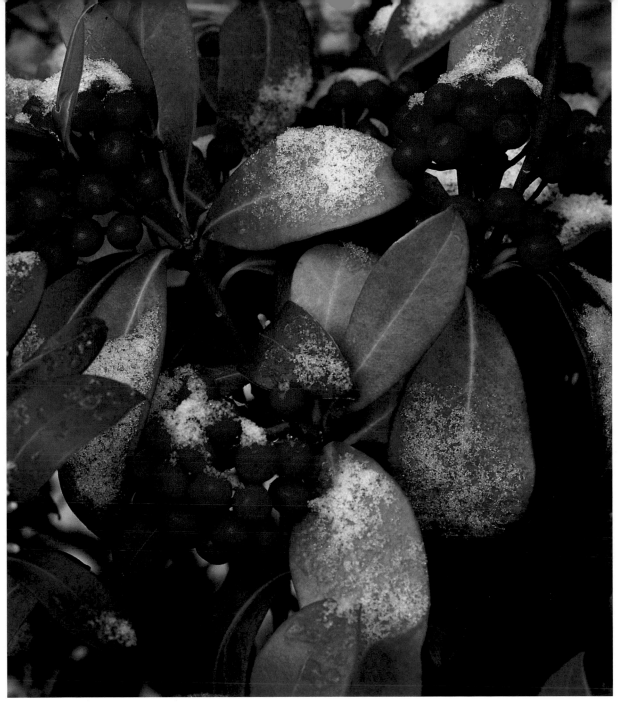

1838, had all these qualities, together with power-fully perfumed flowers, and it would grow in the densely shaded back yards of close-packed houses. It will, of course, do far better in the woodland garden. Put it beside a seat, for the end of a winter afternoon stroll.

Viburnum VIBURNUM, GUELDER ROSE

The guelder rose (*Viburnum opulus*), or 'pliant meally tree' as it was called in the eighteenth century, flowers in winter; in autumn it bears trusses of scarlet or yellow berries and the leaves colour richly. No wonder it was in all old gardens from the sixteenth century and earlier, and in wildernesses from the late seventeenth. It should be in all modern ones too. *V. tinus*, the well-known evergreen laurustinus, shares the same history, though it was often grown in pots to perfume the hall or orangery in winter. Outdoors, in all but the coldest gardens, it makes dense bushes of glittering, dark green leaves, a perfect foil for the autumn colours of maples and cherries.

Above left: Many of the spindles colour well in autumn; this is *Euonymus europaeus*, popular in 'wilderness' gardens for two centuries.

Above right: Skimmia's brilliant berries last through the winter, soon to be followed by a new crop of heavily scented flowers.

Above: Dandelion (*Taraxacum* spp.) and sorrel (*Rumex acetosa*) look quite as fine in fruit as in flower.

Right: A mown path makes it easy to view the flowers and the wildlife without having to wade through dense vegetation.

The whole area soon attracted some less garden-worthy wildlife, for a local deer herd found their way in and discovered that there was excellent grazing to be had among the hedges and the wild plants. They had, reluctantly, to be fenced out, and though the owner doesn't like the appearance of the deer fences, they do allow the meadow to grow. Given a few more seasons undisturbed by intruders the hedge plants will screen the fence from view.

Now that the planting is complete, different areas have slightly different maintenance: one is mown fairly regularly (though buttercups and daisies flower happily); another, the 'spring meadow', is first cut in mid to late July to allow the cowslips and bluebells to flower and seed. Even then, it is cut high enough to allow the cowslips to grow on without losing their leaves. The area also has a scattering of wild daffodils (*Narcissus pseudonarcissus*), cultivated hybrids and

Right: Scabious (*Knautia arvensis*), cornflower (*Centaurea cyanus*), marjoram (*Origanum* spp.) and St John's wort (*Hypericum* spp.) give rich hues and rich food for caterpillars.

snowdrops (*Galanthus nivalis*, grown at least since medieval times), all of which thrive, though crocuses and tulips dwindle in the wet conditions.

The biggest area is devoted to the 'hay meadows', where the different cutting regimes produce distinct floras. Two areas are cut in spring in alternate years, in order to allow butterfly larvae to survive and encourage some plant species, like the southern marsh orchid (*Dactylorhiza praeter-missa*), the handsome and poisonous belladonna (*Atropa belladonna*), wild marjoram, various catch-flies and celandines, cuckoo flower and the bronzy gold flowered *Pilosela aurantiaca*, introduced to Elizabethan gardens from southern Europe and now widely naturalized. Also grown here are wild forms of *Geranium pratense*. Many antique culti-vated forms exist too – look for the gorgeous seventeenth-century doubles.

At the edges of the meadowland, where it comes under the influence of the woodland boundary, the owners have planted foxgloves and the old red campion, often painted in medieval manuscripts and with a pretty double form in gardens since the 1600s at least: a good idea to copy. The meadow is close to the house, but so that the flowers can be seen without tramping though long grass, new shoots and seedlings, a number of paths are cut through the grass and mown frequently; they make pleasant, unmuddy walks at any time of year.

All this comes in return for some extremely hard work at the outset, but thereafter all that is required is one or two mowings a year and some occasional extra effort to make sure that stinging nettles and creeping thistle do not invade and crowd out the more valuable plants.

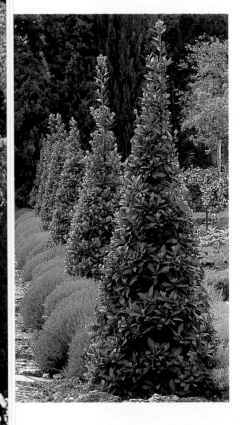

Laurus BAY

Laurus nobilis is the laurel of the Ancients, used to crown poets and heroes, and sacred to Apollo and Aesculapius, god of medicine. Its wonderfully aromatic leaves, smelling of cloves, nutmeg and citrus, have always been admired. It was planted extensively throughout the Roman Empire, for religious as well as culinary reasons, and must have been brought to northern Europe during Roman times. It presumably survived reasonably well, though tough northern winters can easily kill it to the roots.

In medieval times, gardens were frequently designed around a well or fountain, or a central tree. The tree was quite commonly a bay, the traditional symbol of constancy and a popular evergreen. The garden mentioned in Chaucer's poem 'Complaint of Fair Anelida and False Arcite' has both – a well 'that stood under a laurer always green'. Bay must have been taken to America with the early shipments of bulbs in the late seventeenth century and it was certainly grown in nineteenth-century American conservatories.

As for holly, clip bay using secateurs: it's slower than electric shears, but there won't be too many damaged leaves. If you want to ensure you have something for the kitchen, check the plant you are buying. Individuals differ in the strength of their savour; several seedlings in my garden, from the same tree in Rome, smell with differing intensities.

There is a reasonably attractive gold-leafed bay, at its most handsome in the spring, dingy thereafter. It is slightly hardier than the normal form.

Taxus YEW

The yew for the antique garden is *Taxus baccata*, found wild from Northern Europe to the Himalayas, and in North Africa too. It is tough and extremely long-lived – many European gardens boast of having yew trees a thousand years old, though some of them may be much older still.

The basic species is best for both hedge and topiary. The horizontal nature of the branchlets, giving a dense side growth to tall topiaries, allows a marvellous velvety quality if kept in trim. The antique Irish yew (*Taxus baccata* 'Fastigiata') – it was discovered at the end of the eighteenth century – has branchlets which will grow vertically if allowed to do so. The plant is often used to make quick obelisks, but the structure of branching and branchlet gives a much less attractive finish, and mature specimens fall apart under snow. 'Golden' variants (more a sickly yellow) appeared in the mid-nineteenth century.

Taxus baccata makes topiary easily, though the results can be overpowering when they are very large, so they are best suited to large gardens. Young plants, well fed, can grow around 30cm (12in) in a season.

Opposite above: Cones of clipped bay make emphatic statements amongst softer plantings; as its growth is fairly open, large-scale designs are easier to accomplish.

Opposite below: The classic yew, with its dense and hardy growth, is the most flexible of topiary plants, making everything from perfectly plain and architectural hedges to playful designs like this.

Left: The low box hedges that form this parterre and edge the garden paths give shape and structure to the planting.

PLANTS FOR KNOTS AND PARTERRES

The form of the 'knot garden', which began to appear in the early sixteenth century, varied slightly over the two centuries or so of its popularity, but even at its simplest it was a complicated and almost always symmetrical pattern of low, interwoven hedges. Some knots were so dense that the 'infill' areas were left empty or were gravelled. As the fashion progressed, knots became more open; the areas between the hedging were used to plant small flowers like the smaller bulbs, daisies, pinks, violets and strawberries. Taller plants, big enough to interfere with the view of the overall design – which was seen best from the house, or the walk along enclosing walls, or from a garden pavilion – were grown elsewhere.

The 'parterre' garden had many forms. They began to appear in the seventeenth century, when the fascination with mere pattern-making had relaxed rather, and the emphasis shifted strongly to the cultivation of all the new flowers arriving in Western Europe, for which there was not enough room in the old 'knots'. The word 'parterre' merely denotes patterns of plantable earth cut into grass, or box- or lavender-edged beds with gravel paths between, the better to allow examination of the flowers. Parterres after 1820 were often adventurously shaped; contemporary garden magazines ran letters from gardeners horrified by monstrous lapses of taste, having seen a caterpillar parterre or one with butterfly- or tadpole-shaped beds.

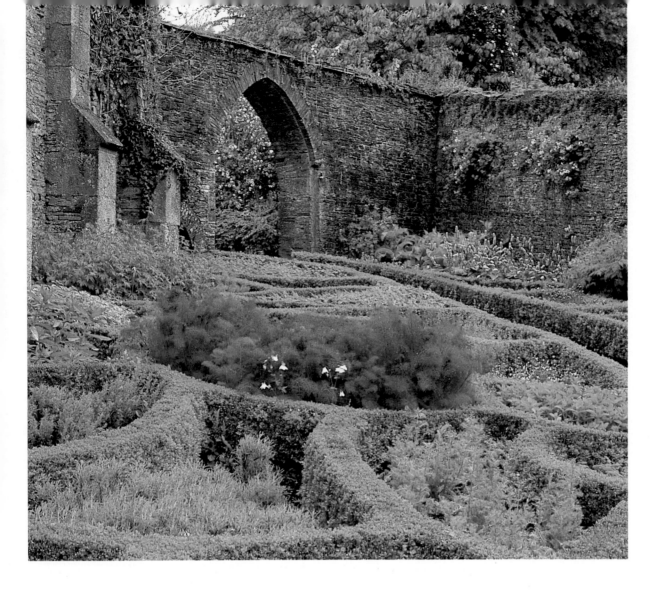

Opposite above: Cones of clipped bay make emphatic statements amongst softer plantings; as its growth is fairly open, large-scale designs are easier to accomplish.

Opposite below: The classic yew, with its dense and hardy growth, is the most flexible of topiary plants, making everything from perfectly plain and architectural hedges to playful designs like this.

Left: The low box hedges that form this parterre and edge the garden paths give shape and structure to the planting.

PLANTS FOR KNOTS AND PARTERRES

The form of the 'knot garden', which began to appear in the early sixteenth century, varied slightly over the two centuries or so of its popularity, but even at its simplest it was a complicated and almost always symmetrical pattern of low, interwoven hedges. Some knots were so dense that the 'infill' areas were left empty or were gravelled. As the fashion progressed, knots became more open; the areas between the hedging were used to plant small flowers like the smaller bulbs, daisies, pinks, violets and strawberries. Taller plants, big enough to interfere with the view of the overall design – which was seen best from the house, or the walk along enclosing walls, or from a garden pavilion – were grown elsewhere.

The 'parterre' garden had many forms. They began to appear in the seventeenth century, when the fascination with mere pattern-making had relaxed rather, and the emphasis shifted strongly to the cultivation of all the new flowers arriving in Western Europe, for which there was not enough room in the old 'knots'. The word 'parterre' merely denotes patterns of plantable earth cut into grass, or box- or lavender-edged beds with gravel paths between, the better to allow examination of the flowers. Parterres after 1820 were often adventurously shaped; contemporary garden magazines ran letters from gardeners horrified by monstrous lapses of taste, having seen a caterpillar parterre or one with butterfly- or tadpole-shaped beds.

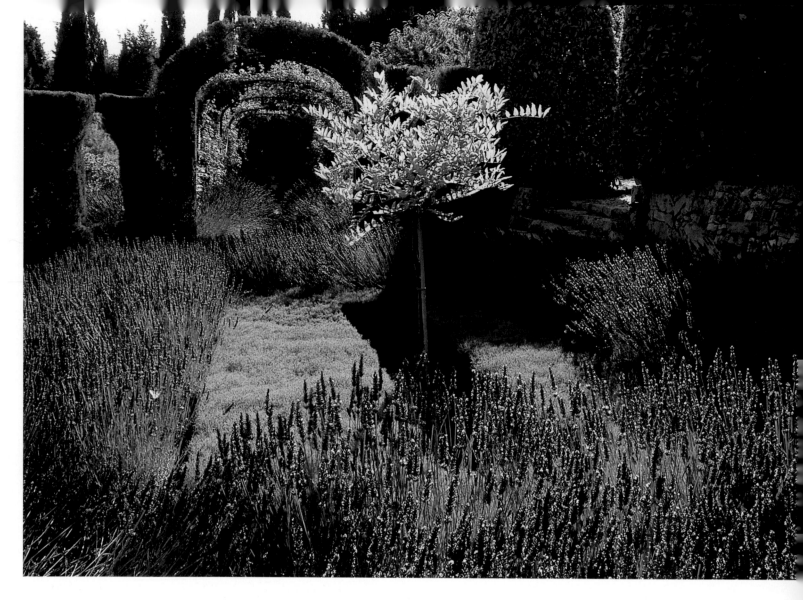

Above: Masses of lavender, here left unclipped and allowed to flower, fill a topiary garden with one of the most evocative of all garden perfumes.

Fagus BEECH

As an alternative to the plants described on pages 80-82, beech can make a glorious hedge around a parterre. Sheared twice a year the common beech (*Fagus sylvatica*) reaches almost any height – 9m (30ft) was once common, and examples can still be found. Such large hedges were used to make extremely grand allées as at Versailles, sometimes trained into elaborate arches as at the astonishing garden at Beloeil in Belgium, where beech, hornbeam and lime have been used to create theatrical views in quite small spaces. The gardens, laid out in the early nineteenth century, are filled with canals and ponds, and the screens of tall greenery and the clusters of gloriettes (several times taller than the ones created by apple trees on page 130) are reflected in the still water.

But clipped beeches can also be used in more domestic spaces, to enclose flower or kitchen gardens, or even a wilderness as at Courances in France. In more modest gardens, they were often pruned into big drums, sometimes on either side of the main gate. In the eighteenth century, there were popular white and yellow variegated sorts, both of which can still be found – as *Fagus sylvatica* 'Albomarginata' and *F. sylvatica* 'Luteovariegata' respectively. The purple *F. sylvatica* 'Purpurea' and its many forms seem to be nineteenth-century varieties and are commonly seen in Victorian woodlands. They can be hedged, though to my mind they are far too heavy a colour and are certainly not to everyone's taste. Bear in mind that beeches are shallow rooted, and tall hedges can dry the soil nearby.

Lavandula LAVENDER

A genus with several species from around the Mediterranean, the hardiest being *Lavandula angustifolia*, used by the Romans and brought by them to northern Europe. It was in every garden from at least the sixteenth century, yielding essential oils for perfumery and medicine, as well as purely garden pleasures. By late medieval times it was used for low hedges in knot gardens and later in parterres. Though all these need clipping to keep them neat, the plants must have been allowed to flower (the young flowerheads are the 'crop' for distillation), for a number of flower variants were grown by the late sixteenth century. Gerard grew the handsome white-flowered *Lavandula angustifolia* 'Alba'.

The usual blue lavender had crossed the Atlantic by the seventeenth century, though it needed protection from cold North American winters. A lovely pink-flowered variant called 'Rosea' or 'Hidcote Pink' is probably recent.

Rosmarinus ROSEMARY

Rosmarinus officinalis was used by the ancient Romans, who associated it with fidelity in love and thought, and made garlands and coronets from it. They may have introduced it into Britain, where it is mentioned in eleventh-century manuscripts. Sir Thomas More wrote, in the early sixteenth century, 'As for Rosemary, I lette it run all over my garden walls, not onlie because my bees love it, but because it is the herbe sacred to remembrance and therefore to friendship...' In the next century the great English botanist John Parkinson grew three kinds, including the 'gilded rosemary' (still around, but much less good-looking than it sounds). Rosemary had reached America by the seventeenth century; white- and pink-flowered sorts (*R. officinalis* 'Albus' and *R. officinalis* 'Majorca Pink'

respectively) were available in the nineteenth. In northern states, rosemary was treated as a greenhouse or conservatory plant.

All can be pruned to make excellent low hedges, say 60–90cm (2–3ft) high and as much deep. They are especially good as hedges in the rose garden; brushing against them as you sniff the roses adds a good base note to the 'bouquet' of the grander flowers, and also gives you something to smell when the roses are over.

Santolina COTTON LAVENDER

Cotton lavender (*Santolina chamaecyparissus*) has been gardened all over Europe since at least 1548, and probably long before. Of Mediterranean origin, it is hardy in much of northern Europe, but even so it may have been rare in Britain; Gerard wrote that it was a smart plant, used 'to border knots with'. By the eighteenth century it was used to edge walks.

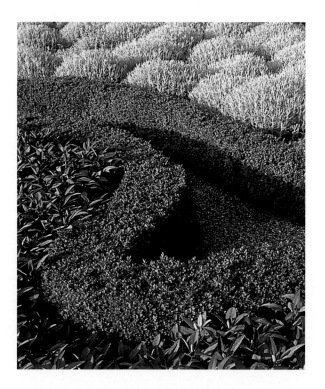

Above: Rosemary, particularly the white-flowered form, clips well into hedges or low obelisks.

Below: Beech holds its warm, rusty brown foliage well into the gales of late winter, giving rich colour to the topiary garden.

Left: Silvery santolina foliage, kept well trimmed, contrasts brilliantly with box hedging; the lower bed is filled with purple-leafed sage (*Salvia officinalis*).

A TOPIARY GARDEN

This garden, enclosed in a rectangle formed by barns and an old farmhouse, was created from what was almost a wilderness about 20 years ago. It has reached something approaching its present form only within the last few years, and is slowly being developed and extended. Much of it is formal in conception and there are topiary elements throughout; the small section shown here is made up almost entirely of topiary and heavily pruned apple trees.

Left: Box is one of the most disciplined of topiary plants, holding its clipped shape well. Trimmed and untrimmed plants side by side are neat without being overly regimental.

Below: Topiary doesn't have to be flamboyant. These carefully trimmed 'tables' make their own subtle statement.

Owned by a famous interior designer, and with early planning and planting input from an equally well-known garden designer, the garden was intended to include many visual references to the owners' personal life, using Mediterranean, Middle and Far Eastern colours and forms (and occasional artefacts), some ancient plants such as yew, myrtle and box, intense variations of light and shade, and ideas taken from classical gardens of seventeenth- and eighteenth-century Italy and France.

While the whole garden is an essay in the various uses of simple topiary forms, it is not in the least in the cottage-garden style. The garden uses topiary in ways which are both stylish and innovative. It is also steeped in visual imagination, from the contemplative 'rill garden' – surrounded by dark yew hedges but with its central pebbled area enclosed by the artificial stream, the stones moistened just enough to ensure that they develop their most sumptuous colours – to marvellously planted pots and tubs.

The most immediate visual impact in the enclosed, almost cloisterish garden is given by the large rectangles of topiary which were all, in the original plans, flat. The subtle low obelisks add a

satisfying new twist to the look of the beds, powerfully framed as several of them are with double outer hedges.

Side sections of clipped box form a grid or very simplified parterre, enclosing silvery clipped tufts of *Santolina chamaecyparissus*, which makes a fine contrast to the box. The santolinas get several clippings through the season to discourage the garish yellow flowers.

Above: Topiary looks best in an enclosed space, whether the enclosing is done by yew hedging or the walls of the house. The area need not be small, but the impact of the planting is spoiled if the garden is allowed to blend into the outside world.

Left: Seen from the house, the enclosed space, filled with its low hedges of clipped box, radiates order and serenity.

Right: As a counterpoint to the trim topiary, the further part of the garden has apple trees, pruned into dramatic shapes, and with irregular flagstones set into the grass beneath them.

Below: Flanking the fine seat are pots of *Acanthus spinosus* and clipped box, symmetrically placed and drawing all the elements of the garden into a cohesive whole.

The box itself is pruned two or three times during the year, using a double-sided hedge-trimmer. The small hedges that form the parterre are easy enough to maintain, but the flat 'tables' of box are more difficult to trim. The gardener simply wades in between the plants (originally arranged at 30cm/1ft intervals) and prunes each table with the help of a very accurate eye. Once the clippings have been roughly brushed off, the box topiary is easily combed back into its usual evenly close-knit surface.

This part of the garden has such a dramatic impact that it takes a moment for the visitor to see the further garden, subtly closed off at the sides by yew buttresses and containing a theatre troupe of apple trees, ten in all, arms raised, in double rows on each side of a flagstone path set flush with the grass. The neat cushion of greenery at the base of each is *Hebe rakaiensis*; this is lightly trimmed, and replaced every few seasons as it gets ragged enough to spoil the effect.

The apples are pruned as the beginnings of arches, while two groups of four at the front link up to make a pair of tiny gloriettes. The pruning means work both during the winter and also just past midsummer when the fruit has set, when excess foliage needs to be cleared away to let light to the fruit. The owner would like a much denser growth of branches, to provide heavier shade and stronger contrasts with the adjacent areas of the garden. If this is to happen, both grass and hebes will suffer and that section of the garden will need to be fundamentally rethought.

There are also some splendid contrasts between yew hedges (often 3–5m/10–16ft high) trimmed into architectural shapes, and grand foliage shrubs, left unpruned, placed in front to give luxuriant effects. Viburnums, with magnificently pleated and veined leaves (*Viburnum rhytidophyllum* would substitute for the unobtainable one grown here), look particularly good, while the pea and jade green *Euphorbia characias* 'Wulfenii' and less spectacular species such as the variegated spiraeas and privets are shown to great advantage. Elsewhere, domes of clipped box sit at the front of beds, like theatre footlights amongst borders billowing with antique roses and ivies.

Although they are not immediately apparent in the photographs, the garden contains some other interesting plantings. As well as the sumptuous

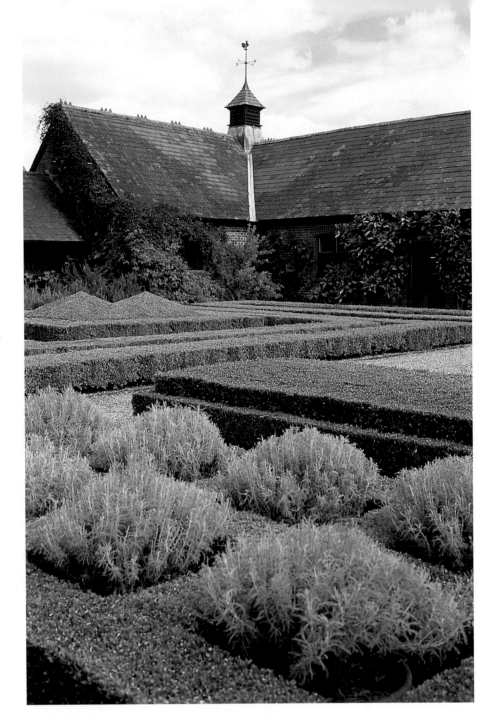

pots of agapanthus, morning glories and clipped myrtles, there are pots of *Acanthus spinosus* for summer foliage and flower spikes, but with the white-veined foliage of *Arum italicum* 'Pictum' for late winter and spring (the foliage dies away in summer). The combination is splendid.

Whatever the future developments of this garden, right now it has great presence. Bear in mind, though, that this sort of garden demands high maintenance. None of it is suitable for the time-pressed gardener.

Above: Domes of silvery *Santolina chamaecyparissus* push out from a grid of clipped box; these two plants have been used together since at least the sixteenth century.

THE ROSE GARDEN

The rose is one of the oldest garden plants. There are references to rose oils, made from petals steeped in almond or olive oils, on clay tablets in the library at Nineveh, destroyed in 612BC. In Greece around 1100BC rose oil was already used for perfume and to embalm the dead. The eastern Mediterranean region possesses many rose species, but *Rosa alba* and *R. gallica*, with their splendid scents, were probably the earliest to be cultivated.

Roses used for chaplets in Egyptian tombs dating from around 100AD seem to be of a lovely hybrid which can still be grown: *Rosa sancta*, now called *R. x richardii*. In ancient Rome, roses were worn as wreaths for the head, to cool the brow and keep smell and disease at bay; they were used as flavourings for food, in ointments and perfumes, and to bury the dead. The rich slept on pillows of rose petals, and the Emperor Heliogabalus is supposed to have suffocated some unfortunate dinner guests in vast mounds of petals dropped from the ceiling of a banqueting pavilion.

Left: The antique rose 'Blairii No. 2', here combined with the more recent 'Fleurette' and a white clematis, makes a gorgeous perfumed cascade. Above: Shrub roses are tough and long-lived. This one, painted by Redouté for the Empress Josephine, seems to have vanished, but may, like many others, still survive in old gardens.

Naturally, such demand for roses necessitated a huge cultivation of them, and the island of Rhodes was famous for its rose production. It is not clear how many roses the Romans grew, but they probably had the lovely *Rosa* 'Alba Maxima', a double form of *R. gallica*, and *R. damascena*. Each of these went on to give rise to whole groups of varieties, which have survived through the centuries and still have many representatives today. However, as many nineteenth-century roses are complicated crosses between all these groups, they are very much obscured by the hundreds of intermediate types and, in many cases, it is impossible to ascribe a rose variety to any of them. This is no disadvantage, for even if it were possible the classification tells the gardener very little about the qualities of any particular variety.

New roses gradually developed in the East, and reached the West along trade routes, or were brought back by Crusaders. In early medieval Persia, rose gardens feature in much poetry, especially that of Sa'di (1194–1296AD), for whom a *Gulistan* is both a rose garden and a collection of poems. In Persia the

Opposite: Redouté's painting of 'Rosa indica', probably the variety now called 'Rosier des Indes', whcih is still grown at Malmaison in France.

Below: An Edwardian rose garden in autumn, with hybrid tea roses in flower.

double yellow form of *Rosa hemisphaerica* (syn. *R. lutea*), which arrived in Britain in 1583, was often worn behind the ear, given as a present or used for rose water. In the East, too, garden plants were collected, especially by Al Mu'tasim at Samarra in modern Iraq, where there was an extensive rose collection. Not surprisingly, roses figure strongly in garden descriptions in *The Arabian Nights* (whose stories were probably first collected in the twelfth century).

Roses grown in princely Europe, native species as well as ones treasured in ancient Rome, can be seen on the page borders of medieval psalters and prayer books. The species depicted is often the wild dog rose, but there are also red, pale pink and white 'cabbage' types. It was common in Italian and French gardens of the thirteenth and fourteenth centuries to find vines, roses and water, all reflecting the mathematics, geometry, symbolism and philosophical ideas from the Near East. Boccaccio's *Decameron* describes the Villa Palmieri, where the ladies sheltered from city plague. There, 'with several walks and alleys long and spacious..., covered with spreading vines, whereon the grapes hung in copious clusters, and surrounded by white and red roses and jasmines...', the perfumes protected them from infection.

In Islamic Spain of the same period, roses were grown more imaginatively: at the Alcazar, there are still fragments of 'gloriettas' left: arbours of cypress, twined with roses and jasmine, and used for dining. In Northern India, Shah Jahan built the island garden of the Four Plane Trees, square, of half an acre (about 2,000 sq.m) and planted entirely with roses, stocks, marigolds and vines – a planting easily copied today. An interesting colour scheme, too, for he had something new: a rose called 'Dou Roux' with petals red on one side, copper yellow on the other and so rare that feasts were planned for its blooming. It may have been *Rosa foetida* 'Bicolor', still found and looking astonishing among modern marigolds.

A few medieval roses exist: the white *Rosa alba* in single and double forms, the red *R. gallica officinalis*, the dog rose (*R. canina*), the damask rose (*R. damascena*) and wild varieties such as the eglantine and *R. arvensis* (the only one that can be used as a climber). There were scarcely more Renaissance roses, and only nine garden sorts known in Holland or Britain by 1684. Widely admired were the 'cabbage' roses belonging to the species *R. × centifolia*, soon to appear in many Dutch flower paintings, and which had probably been recently introduced from Constantinople, despite the fact that it was called the Provence rose. Genetic analysis suggests that it had a complex parentage, being descended from 'gallica', 'damask', 'dog', 'musk' and Phoenician roses. It, too, went on swiftly to establish a large number of subsidiary varieties.

Renaissance and seventeenth-century roses still in gardens include the charming *Rosa majalis,* still commonly sold under its former name of *R. cinnamomea*; *R. × francofurtana*, now often found under the more recent name 'Empress Josephine'; the extraordinary *R. gallica* 'Versicolor', which is often called *R. mundi*, striped and splashed in two shades of pink; the yellow *R. hemisphaerica*; the double-flowered *R. moschata*; and the very first American rose, *R. virginiana*.

Rose breeding took off in the 1780s and every season saw new varieties. The introduction, in 1786, of the four Chinese floribunda-type roses, with their double flowering season, gave a great impetus to the rose industry. The crosses with European types gave rise to the hardy perpetual roses that were in flower from early summer to the first frosts. However, new sorts of rose continued to pour in from America, India and China, all at once used for breeding.

But the reverse happened too, to make the evolutionary story more complicated, and the new European varieties were being shipped, potted, to Carolina by 1732, and to China soon after. In their new homes, the roses were crossed with native species, or into varieties that had arrived earlier.

By 1831, the colossal *General System of Gardening and Botany* by David Don, intended to list every plant grown in European gardens, named, but didn't describe, 211 Scotch roses, 54 damasks, 68 centi-folias and 706 other roses probably belonging to the centifolia group – almost all with French names. Among these were the ones painted by Redouté, to capture the new glories for one of the most illustrious of rose collectors, the Empress Josephine. Once married to Napoleon, and once he was emperor, Josephine set about making their modest country retreat at Malmaison into a more fitting house. She seems to have been a keen and interested gardener and, falling in love with the new roses of the early nineteenth century, she had assembled a world-famous collection by the time of her death in 1814.

Many Victorian roses survive: a number of the moss roses, the wonderful *Rosa* 'Souvenir de la Malmaison' (widely grown as a potted rose and still excellent though, alas, bred twenty years after Josephine's death), *R.* 'Gloire de Dijon', *R.* 'Louise Odier' and many others. Indeed, most of what we now call the 'old' roses date from around 1850 or so and are of French provenance.

So exciting was the huge wave of introductions of new species and the breeding of new varieties that by 1800 many gardeners found that they had to have an area in their gardens entirely devoted to roses, in order to grow even a fraction of the marvellous innovations. By the middle of the century, the rose was probably the most fashionable flower of all.

The Victorian 'rosarium' was the subject of debate: there were innumerable popular layouts, but one of the commonest was to have a large circular bed divided into segments, one for each variety or group. Rose beds were often edged with half-hardy bedding plants, wallflowers or tiny annuals, so that there was still something to look at once the main rose-flowering season was over. Vertical emphasis, where needed, could be given by trellis-work obelisks or arches, supporting new climbing varieties.

Some Victorian gardeners tried rather more daring ways of growing some of the weaker-stemmed bush roses, particularly the 'basket of roses': circular or rectangular beds, often almost 2m (6ft) across, edged with wire basketwork 45cm (18in) tall. The earth inside was built up into a mound 60cm (2ft) high, a number of plants of one variety were put in and, as they grew, their stems were arched down and pegged to the earth. Eventually the desired effect – a tight and floriferous cone of roses – was formed.

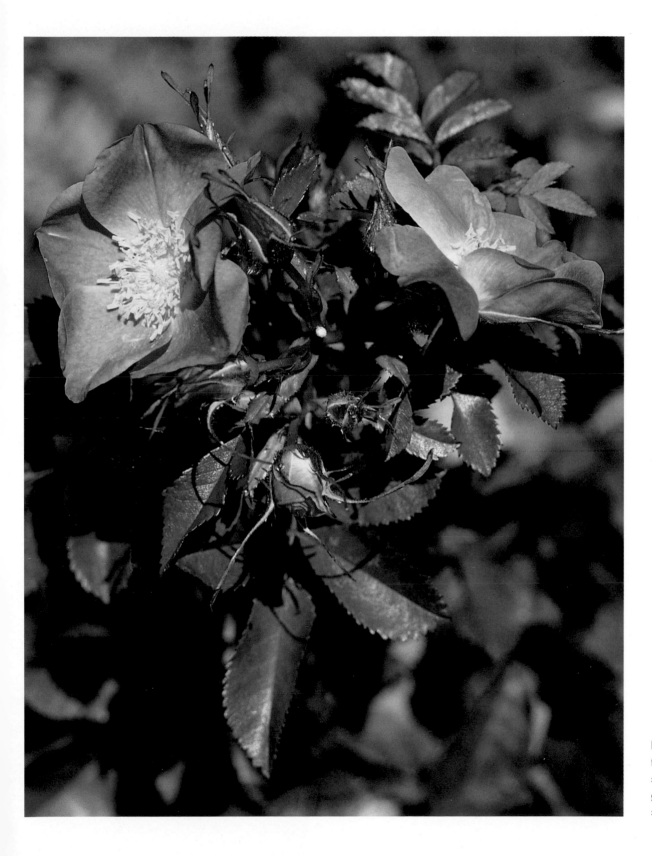

Left: *Rosa virginiana*,
the first of the American
species to reach European
gardens; it arrived in the
seventeenth century.

SHRUB ROSES

Most shrub roses have stems that are rarely more than 1.5m (4ft 6in) long, though *Rosa* 'Alba Maxima' can reach 2m (6ft 6in) or more. Stems can be thin and floppy, making a spreading bush (as in *R.* 'Fantin Latour'), or thicker and upright, making the bush a good deal tidier. Though the individual flowers of old shrub roses look perfect, some varieties can flop badly when the weight of flowers is heaviest. It is worth making low frames or rustic poles around each bush, with crossbars about 90cm (3ft) above ground level. This will keep the flowers well above other plants and let you see and smell them without too much effort.

The growth habit of many old roses means that it is easy to fill the ground beneath them with plants that appreciate the shade. Forms of the lesser periwinkle (*Vinca minor*), with their dark green, glossy leaves, make a good contrast, but if you want more diversity, include ferns, violas – especially the variants of *Viola cornuta*, which look wonderful with the sharp pinks of many old roses – ivies, some pale yellow foxgloves such as *Digitalis grandiflora* and *D. lutea,* and forms of *Campanula persicifolia.* That association of plants suits almost all old roses, even the darkest reds.

In very cold areas, not all roses are winter hardy, and some of the ones with Chinese and Indian species in their blood can be grown extremely well in the conservatory or greenhouse. Some of the Banksian roses are perfect for the back wall in a cold climate, but try some of the shrub sorts in large pots too. Many do well, producing much larger flowers under glass and flowering much earlier in the season. As many old roses have a short season of flower, having them in pots means that they can also be grown on out of the way, when flowering is finished.

Below: The flowers of *Rosa eglanteria*, in soft pink, are followed by innumerable hips in a curious rusty red, but the real reason why the eglantine rose is essential in the garden lies in its leaves. Fresh ones have a powerful smell of apples cooking, especially strong just after rain, and that delicious perfume wafts around the garden.

Rosa 'Alba Maxima'

Sometimes called the Jacobite rose, this variety is certainly older than that cause, dating from at least the early seventeenth century. The Romans seem to have had a double *Rosa alba*, though it may have been the one called *R.* 'Semiplena'. All are disease free, tough, free flowering and quite large. Plant them at the back of your border or on rustic tripods as the centrepieces to rose beds.

Rosa eglanteria EGLANTINE

This is the eglantine of Shakespeare and was probably grown in the ancient world. It was also one of the first European species to reach America, when Dutch settlers planted seed in the gardens of New Holland. They can hardly have wanted it for its flowers. However, it makes a marvellous hedge, either left to do as it will, in which case it needs about 2.5m (8ft) of garden, or roughly trimmed once or twice a season, when it rapidly makes an impenetrable barrier to all but the smallest creatures. In the eighteenth century branches were commonly cut to put among other flowers in a bowl in the hall or parlour. If you need a rose hedge with more flowers, add some of the Scots briars, which are equally tough but have enchanting blooms, often exquisitely scented.

Rosa 'Empress Josephine'

Illustrated in 1820, this wonderful rose flowers, in quantity, on a pretty, almost thornless bush. It is in fact older than the early nineteenth century: under its earlier name of *Rosa francofurtana* it dates back at least to the 1580s, and may be older even than that. Certainly the first one in British gardens was imported by John Tradescant the Elder, who collected it in Frankfurt in 1618, while accompanying an English ambassador journeying to Russia. The smell is good too.

Left: Despite the name, *Rosa* 'Alba Maxima' is not quite white, for the young flowers have a pinkish glow, but it is perhaps one of the oldest doubles.

Above: *Rosa* 'Empress Josephine' is richly double, and a marvellous sharp pink with deeper and stronger overtones.

Rosa foetida

Native to western Asia, this is the species that brought yellow – and susceptibility to black spot – into rose breeding. One form, *Rosa foetida* 'Bicolor', has sumptuous single flowers, with petals that are copper-rose coloured on the inside, mustardy yellow without. It has been known in the East since the twelfth century at least, and in the West since the sixteenth. Persian writers called it the 'Dou Roux' rose, and feasts were held among its flowers. The form called 'Persiana' is all yellow, and double: it reached Western Europe in 1837, to much acclaim.

Rosa × 'Harison's Yellow'

Though popularly called the Yellow Rose of Texas and sometimes given a species name of *Rosa × harisonii*, this is an 1830 cross between two Europeans – the ancient *R. foetida* and the little Scots rose *R. pimpinellifolia*. Making a bigger shrub than either, it seems to have been carried westward with the settlers' migration, so, unlike *R. pimpinellifolia*, it must 'take' easily as cuttings. It is both handsome and hardy. Keep it away from pink old roses, planting it amongst irises, astrantias, the blue-green flowered *Penstemon glabra* or *P.* 'Alice Hindley', and *Alchemilla mollis*.

Rosa 'Ispahan'

Gorgeous, sharpish pink, packed with petals, marvellously perfumed, disease free, *R.* 'Ispahan' adds to its virtues by having a longer season than many other old roses. It has been known since 1832 and may have originated in the city of its name. It looks well with *Rosa* 'Maiden's Blush' and *R.* 'Madame Hardy'. The growth is lax and, unsupported, it makes a perfect rose to sprawl downwards over a low wall, beside a seating area, where you can easily sniff its delicious flowers. Underplant it with a mix of pale blue *Viola cornuta* and periwinkles.

Rosa 'Madame Hardy'

The purest white flowers of this rose are cooled still further by a tiny central boss of green, showing only when the magnificent flower is fully open. The perfume is rich, but similarly cool. The whole plant, first recorded in 1832, exudes style, is a strong grower and soon makes a fine large bush. Along with 'Madame Legras de St Germain', it is one of the most beautiful of the white roses. Grow it among pink-flowered lavenders, clumps of lungworts and artemisias.

Opposite above: *Rosa foetida* 'Persiana' – in the West since 1837 – is all yellow and delightfully double.

Opposite below: *Rosa* x 'Harison's Yellow' – the Yellow Rose of Texas – is in fact of nineteenth-century European origin.

Centre: The green 'eye' at the centre of *Rosa* 'Madame Hardy' makes the flower seem even whiter. The perfume is delicious, too.

Above right: The tidy habit of *Rosa* 'Ispahan' means that it looks perfect by the path or terrace and it won't flop to impede your walk.

Below right: The scent of *Rosa* 'Madame Isaac Periere' pours from large, blowsy flowers, which start out a strong cerise pink and age rapidly to a greyer tone.

Rosa 'Madame Isaac Pereire'

Dating from 1881, this provides one of the great perfumes of the garden. Powerful stems and foliage make it easy to look after, and it has a scattering of blooms into autumn. I grow it along a rustic fence by my kitchen garden, where valerians, white-fruited strawberries and the black-flowered *Iris chrysographes* 'Black Knight' are also planted. However, it is powerful enough to be allowed to clamber up a wall or into an apple tree, where it can look excellent. The banker to whom the immortal Madame Pereire was married eventually bankrupted himself.

Above: Rosa mundi,
with its gorgeously striped
petals and luscious smell,
has to be in every collection
of antique roses.

Rosa 'Maiden's Blush'

'Maiden's Blush' is of tough constitution, though not of buxom stature. A lovely cottage rose, popular all over Europe, it is certainly medieval, perhaps older still. It looks good against a green background, half-engulfed by *Iris pseudacorus*, hostas and forms of *Geranium pratense*.

Rosa mundi

With its wonderful, lightly double flowers splashed and streaked in two shades of sugar pink, this may be the rose from 'Fair Rosamund's bower' (Rosamund was the mistress of the English king Henry II, and her rose is therefore medieval). However, Sir Thomas Hanmer, writing in the early

Rosa 'Quatre Saisons'

If you miss roses after midsummer, grow this ancient variety, probably the 'twice flowering' rose used in the rites of Aphrodite in Greece in 1000BC and later of Venus in Rome. Prettily pink and very scented, it has been in gardens ever since and is used as a parent of other long-flowering groups. It gives a second wave of flowers, not as strong as the first, in late summer and early autumn. Not big, it should be grown in front of other bush roses, and among 'Old English' lavender, where it looks enchanting. Its blood runs strong in the lovely 'Rose de Rescht', an old Persian variety.

Rosa 'Souvenir de la Malmaison'

Soft pink, with the petals arranged in clearly marked 'quarters', this rose thrives in a hot place in the garden and does even better in a large pot in the conservatory. Being a bourbon – and so with autumn-flowering *Rosa chinensis* as well as summer-flowering 'Damask' in its veins – it has a reasonably long season of flower. It dates from 1843, but the climbing form is modern.

seventeenth century, says that it was a fairly recent 'sport' (a variant which arises from a single bud on a growing bush) from the double *Rosa gallica*, to which an occasional branch of *R. mundi* still returns. Whatever its origins, it is heavily perfumed and makes a splendid low hedge, though it is susceptible to mildew.

Above left: The form of *Rosa* 'Maiden's Blush' usually sold is 'Great Maiden's Blush', shown here. It is a lovely, refreshingly perfumed, soft pink rose with gracefully curled petals.

Above right: *Rosa* 'Souvenir de la Malmaison', sensual and sumptuous, is one of the most magnificent of nineteenth-century roses and deserves grand treatment in the garden.

Below left: Probably one of the most ancient cultivated roses, this variety is now called *Rosa* 'Quatre Saisons', though it has, in fact, only two waves of flowers, the second in late summer.

CLIMBERS

The ramblers, often hybrids of *Rosa wichuraiana*, mainly date from the early twentieth century and are not old enough to be included here. They commonly produce long canes, rather in the manner of raspberries, and flower on second-year canes, which are cut out once flowering is finished. The proper climbers produce canes too, but these keep growing and flowering vigorously. Many climbers are very vigorous indeed (*R. filipes* 'Kiftsgate' can easily grow 4.5–7.5m/15–25ft in a season); they need to be planted with forethought.

Victorian gardeners with exotic inclinations made 'gloriettes', based on Arabic examples; many chose *R.* 'Alba Maxima', which can be treated as a climber. When northern gardeners needed more light than was appropriate in southern Spain – where these arbours were designed to provide much-needed shade – some used groups of metal rose arches and surrounded the structure with lavenders or myrtles to get the lovely resiny perfume on hot afternoons. If you want to do something similar, the double musk rose is still the best, and if your climate won't allow *Jasminum officinale*, use honeysuckles instead.

Good places for climbing roses are sprawling along pergolas (where the large ones can look marvellous), up walls, over outbuildings and up trees. Many climbing roses are, or are bred from, what are in effect lianas. They happily clamber up trees of substantial size, and nothing can look lovelier than an old pear or apple tree swathed with the flowers of *Rosa* 'Paul's Himalayan Musk', an Ayrshire such as *R.* 'Janet B. Wood' or the magnificent *R.* 'The Garland'.

Likewise, a vigorous rose climbing up a wall needs stout wires or hooks to hold it in place, and will need regular thinning if you don't want it to tear loose in a gale or collapse under a weight of snow. Roses that have fallen free are often an impenetrable tangle, and best cut right back to a couple of good stems. They soon start off again. The risk is well worthwhile, for almost nothing looks more romantic than a house, summerhouse or outbuilding half-enveloped in roses.

Pergolas (or arbours) need to be strong enough to support the weight of vegetation, particularly if you want to combine your roses with vines, wisterias, clematis, honeysuckle or jasmine. They also need to be high enough to leave sufficient head room to allow the plants to hang from the beams, but not get in your way as you pass beneath. Although only a rich mixture of plants will produce a truly romantic effect, the tangle will prevent your doing any pruning, so you will need to do more radical work every five or six seasons.

Rosa 'Blairii No. 2'

On a north-facing wall, and with care taken to keep down mildew, this is one of the loveliest of the pink climbers, with flowers of perfect form, petals staying a deeper pink near the centre and a perfume that gives many gardeners the shivers. It provides a few flowers, too, later in summer, and will remind you all over again about how superior old roses are in form, colour and scent to almost any of the 'moderns', even with their tea-rose blood. If you can bear to harvest it, the flowers of this variety cut well and the slightly pendant habit of the flowers works well in a vase. It was first grown in 1845. Don't grow it twined with anything else; let as much air as possible through the foliage. In some seasons you will need to spray it with fungicide. When it is in flower all the work will seem worthwhile.

Opposite: *Rosa* 'Paul's Himalayan Musk' is one of the most vigorous of the climbers, delicately scented and flowering freely in late summer.

Above: *Rosa* 'Blairii No. 2', with its all-pervading perfume, is an ideal rose to go over a small arbour, shading a garden seat.

Above left: On a sheltered wall the semi-evergreen *Rosa* 'Blush Noisette' can be very vigorous, reaching a height of 7m (20ft) in two or three seasons.

Above right: The lightly scented *Rosa* 'Madame Alfred Carrière' carries on flowering well into autumn. Fully hardy, it is a delight for northern gardens.

Rosa 'Blush Noisette'

Extremely vigorous in good soil and on a sunny wall, this rose also does well in less favourable circumstances, and is disease resistant too. From high summer it has big clusters of double, flattish, pale pink flowers, opening from enchanting pinker buds, perfumed with orange peel and spices. It can flower well into autumn and is easy to grow from cuttings. I grow it with white wisteria, and the lovely old vine called 'Incana' or 'Dusty Miller'. The rose was first recorded in 1817.

Rosa 'Félicité et Perpétue'

Almost evergreen in mild gardens, this 1827 rose also flowers later than many climbers, for which it can be forgiven its lack of exciting perfume. Clusters of very double, very pretty, modestly pink flowers can cover the whole plant to dramatic effect. It is hardy, disease free and good on a pergola or screen with vines (*Vitis vinifera* 'Purpurea' looks good) and the pale blue late-flowering *Clematis* × *jouiniana*.

Rosa 'Madame Alfred Carrière'

Famous on the cottage wall at Sissinghurst in Kent, this rose will grow in shade too. Flowers are buff-white when young, proper white later, rather tea-rose shaped, and with that smell too – delicious, and a change from the headier perfumes of older roses. Only just antique at 1879, it is a delight in the garden, with flowers into autumn. I grow it as a backdrop to a planting of pink lavenders and the rose 'Empress Josephine' (see page 97).

Rosa 'The Garland'

Bred in 1835, this is a delightful and very vigorous rose. Red-purple stems and good foliage make it attractive even out of flower. Gertrude Jekyll liked it so much that she used it to swag ropes strung along the verandah of her own house, Munstead Wood in Surrey. There can be no better recommendation. When I was once lucky enough to own an eighteeth-century summerhouse, I planted its walls with this rose, late Dutch honey-suckle and *Jasminum stephanense*.

Above: *Rosa* 'The Garland' has airy clusters of small, amethyst-pink roses, fading as they age and slightly but spicily perfumed.

Left: *Rosa* 'Félicité et Perpétue' is another vigorous climber which copes well with the rigours of autumn. Many of what we now call 'old' roses are of French provenance – this one is named after two otherwise forgotten sisters.

Right: Against an estate cottage wall, climbing roses make an attractive planting combined with *Euphorbia characias* and sweet rocket (*Hesperis matronalis*) beneath.

Below: A single red form of *Rosa rugosa*, growing among cow parsley in a wild part of the garden.

A GARDEN FOR OLD ROSES

This rambling manor house must always have had roses of some sort planted around it, perhaps *Rosa gallica* 'Officinalis' and *R. mundi*, or later *R.* 'Celestial' in pale pink and the tiny deep pink *R.* 'De Meaux'. These would have been part of the general planting, but, in the early 1900s, the house was given a rose garden devoted to their culture. Set a short walk from the house, it is walled off from the rest of the garden, giving it a sense of retreat and privacy.

Left: The walk between
rose arches is paved with
brick, laid to accentuate
the length of the view.

Above: 'New Dawn'
flowers late and does
well in cold gardens.

Below: Although not quite
antique, 'Seagull's' ancient
heritage and beautiful
fragrance earn it a place
in any rose garden.

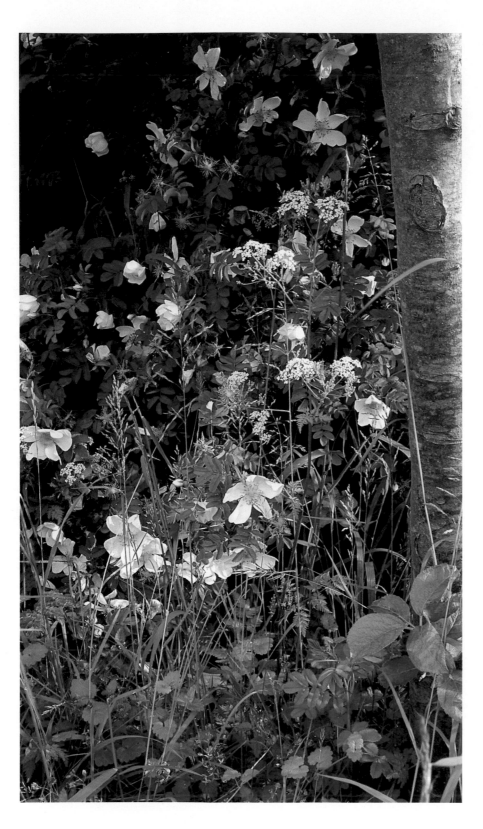

Perhaps the garden once had the wooden trellis-work arches and arbours that were fashionable in the seventeenth century, but these would have been smothered in musk roses, the uprights perhaps covered with *Rosa* 'Alba Maxima'. The present arbour is romantically swathed in dense growths of 'Seagull' and 'New Dawn'. Though 'New Dawn' dates only from the years in which this garden was built, it is a very attractive, easy and constant-flowering derivative of 'Dr W. Van Fleet', an American hybrid raised in 1910.

Alternate arches are planted with the gorgeous and vigorous 'Seagull'. It dates from 1909, so is fast becoming an antique. It is a historic cross, though, one parent being the ancient Chinese species (and favoured garden plant) *Rosa multiflora*. Introduced to Europe at the end of the eighteenth century, *R. multiflora* is a rose worth having in its own right, with huge clusters of white and fragrant flowers. 'Seagull's' other parent was 'General Jacqueminot', a gorgeous hybrid perpetual of 1852, which is still available.

'Seagull' is strongly perfumed and though it has mostly a single season, producing only a few flowers later in the year, even then it will perfume the whole garden and beyond. If you want to plant your own rose arch, you should be able to achieve the same pitch of luxuriance in five or six good growing seasons.

Other roses in this part of the garden are grown with their stems twined around metal obelisks (though some blend even more delicately with structures built from rustic poles). The brightest is the flaming scarlet *Rosa* 'Excelsa', dating from 1909. Flowering sometimes twice a year, this possesses a lot of the characteristics of the Chinese *R. wichuraiana*, while the clustered flower buds come from *R. multiflora*. Although not quite an antique itself, 'Excelsa' therefore has links to two antique climbers. If you like the idea, try it with one of the antique climbers described on pages 102–105. Be warned, though, that only modern roses will give you quite this shade of red.

Elsewhere in the garden, shrub rose bushes have a topiary background, the dark green of the yew hedging making a splendid foil to the wild growth and the sumptuous colours of the roses. It is an effect well worth trying in a much smaller garden, either with topiary elements giving form, summer and winter, to the rose garden, or with the structure being supplied by a backing fence or wall covered with the dark green foliage of ivy.

In yet another part of the garden roses are grown in an entirely informal way, almost as if they were wild bushes, left to make their own way, either as specimens on neatly mown lawn or in long grass. They can look equally romantic in either setting, so an informal rose garden could happily be bordered by – or even blend into – a meadow garden or kitchen garden.

Especially good for this treatment, and well represented in this garden, are some of the 'rugosa' roses. These developed from the Japanese sand-dune species, first in Europe in the 1860s, and used soon after for hybridization. 'Mrs Anthony Waterer' is a good one dating from 1898, but in this garden the dark and sumptuous 'Roseraie de l'Hay' is from 1901, the paler 'Delicata' from 1898 and the handsome double white 'Blanche Double de Coubert' 1892. All have long flowering seasons, do not seem to be troubled by pests and never suffer from black spot. They have strong perfumes and, as they also flower well in the shade of walls and buildings, they make excellent antiques for urban rose gardens.

However, no manor-house garden restricts all its roses to a special rose garden. Elsewhere in this garden, old roses are planted against the walls of

both the service cottages and the house itself. Entirely simple, some of the plantings by the windows are especially attractive. The walls hold 'Zéphirine Drouhin' and 'Madame Alfred Carrière', both easy and beautiful, with a cottage-garden planting beneath of annual poppies, *Artemisia absinthium* 'Lambrook Silver', the perfumed sweet rocket (*Hesperis matronalis*) and the long-lasting greenery of *Euphorbia characias* 'Wulfenii'.

Other parts of these borders contain eye-catching plants such as the silvery-leafed and sky-blue flowered *Teucrium fruticans* and the gawky but pretty Victorian verbena, *Verbena bonariensis*. To complement the generous clumps of woolly-leafed *Stachys byzantina*, try adding an occasional bush of *Rosa* 'Empress Josephine' and a cluster of *R.* 'Ispahan' by the front, or the kitchen, door. On the wall, a less florid rose to try would be the delightful *R.* 'Blairii No. 2'.

Opposite: Wilder parts of the garden are ideal for species roses, like this yellow variant of the Carolina rose.

Left: Evening light makes the rose garden even more romantic.

Above: 'Ethel', a popular, vigorous and easy climber from the early 1900s.

Below: A fairly modern floribunda rose, of a shade of red not found in antique roses, but here bringing a welcome contrast to the whites and pale pinks.

THE KITCHEN GARDEN

This is the most ancient sort of garden. Many fruit plants appear in creation myths: palm, quince, vine and apple, have all been regarded as the cosmic Tree of Life (or Knowledge), growing atop a sacred mount, or in the Garden of Eden, and often associated in some way with snakes. Many kitchen garden plants have been connected with magic and ritual into quite modern times. Kitchen gardens have also been places in which to proclaim status; in 1000BC, a Babylonian king wrote a catalogue of the vegetables, fruit and medicinal herbs in his gardens, and a few centuries later Sennacherib, King of Assyria, thought his so important that he built an aqueduct to carry water to its fruit trees.

Though royal gardens were on colossal scales, Homer describes a rather more domestic one: the gardens of Alcinous, an enclosed area of about 8000 sq.m (4 acres), hedged, with fruit trees planted in regular rows (the first mention of a 'quincunx', a grid planting which remained in use in the West well into the 1700s).

Left: Vegetables, herbs and flowers such as marigolds and nasturtiums blend easily with topiary box and formal paths in this delightful potager. Above: A nineteenth-century turnip from the German Benary seed catalogue. Use old varieties for the varying shades of their leaves. The young foliage and flower shoots are delicious.

In ancient Greece, too, the landscape seems to have been dotted with sacred gardens: an inscription at Thasos describes the lease of a garden devoted to Heracles outside the town, which was to provide figs, hazels and myrtles, and boasted porticos and banqueting rooms.

Gardens of the Roman Empire are better known. Recent excavations of Pompeian houses show that the courtyards were often filled with figs, cherries, apples and pears, probably high pruned in order to allow flowers and vegetables to be grown beneath. Some trees had vines trained up the stems. Roman gardens were still places for the gods, not only those of the household, but the god of the garden, Priapus.

After the fall of Rome the traditions of kitchen gardening continued in monasteries and princely gardens, and probably lower down the social scale. Many kept in at least distant touch with the developing traditions of the Orient, and soon influences from ever further east were reaching Western Europe; in 1404, the court of Tamburlaine, at Samarkand, was visited by the Castilian ambassador. Invited to various receptions in gardens, he was even lodged in one, and described it in disbelieving terms: 'We found it enclosed by a high wall... and within it is full of fruit trees of all kinds save only limes and citrons...' He eventually saw Tamburlaine, seated on a dais in front of an immense fountain, upon whose waters floated scarlet apples.

A century later, the Mughal Emperor Babur wrote his memoirs and included details of many of his most beloved gardens. These, illustrated with paintings commissioned by his son, show watercourses, vegetable beds and bountiful fruit trees to provide shade for banquets.

As the Renaissance moved outwards from Italy a century or so later, so spread a renewed interest in the diversity of plants, and most especially of fruit trees. These were eagerly collected as badges of sophistication, intellectual and gastronomic. In England, Henry VIII and his gardeners are often thought of as having introduced all sorts of new crops to Britain, from Turk's cap pumpkins (brought from Constantinople, though introduced there from central and southern North America), new sorts of greengage, spinach, the first apricot (since Roman times anyway), apples and many others. In late sixteenth-century France, where the first parterres were beginning to evolve, collections of exotic fruit and vegetables had already been formed at the chateau of Blois. The Queen's garden had vegetables planted inside the new box compartments of the great parterres. Further north, Renaissance attitudes gradually enlivened the table; seventeenth-century Scottish and Scandinavian grandees had walls with trained fruit, sometimes terracing the steep site originally chosen for defensive reasons, sometimes using new walls enclosing the front courtyard, so that grand plants could be seen by all visitors. Among other exotica they imported lemon trees from Italy and cauliflower seed from Crete.

Not only Europe and the Near East were being explored for new delicacies; the first American crops reached European shores in the late 1400s, but many more arrived in the succeeding century. These crops (the tomato, the potato, aubergines/eggplant, peppers, maize, squashes and pumpkins) all made a colossal impact on European gardens and kitchens, as well as on the kitchens of the Near East and North Africa. Many of the new crops were so delicious, and so high yielding, that ancient native crops, especially among the root vegetables, began to drop out of use.

The 'show' aspects of vegetable and fruit gardens began to wane just into the eighteenth century, when French influence was increasingly in the ascendant. In Western Europe, the kitchen garden, though still an important part of any large garden, became a separate entity, often a walled enclosure at some distance from the main house. Many were extremely grand.

Extraordinary things were attempted in these gardens; the novelist Daniel Defoe found oranges being grown outdoors on an English estate, at least 800km (500 miles) north of where this is conventionally done: '...and [they] have moving houses [of glass and timber] to cover them in winter; they are loaded with fruit in the summer, and the gardeners told us, they have stood in the ground where they now grow above eighty years...'

Nineteenth-century ingenuity in the kitchen garden went on to produce endless new varieties of important crops, as the scientific aspects of hybridization developed rapidly. Ironically, the same century saw the growth of high-efficiency farming as well as a vast increase in the size of towns and cities. Both meant that most people could buy cheaply varieties bred for farm methods, rather than varieties bred for the more individual needs of gardening enthusiasts. 'Local' varieties, some historic, some modern, became extinct in huge numbers.

Nevertheless, growing the surviving antiques of the kitchen garden can give the gardener, especially of fruit species, crops more delicious and more beautiful than anything that can be bought. Though a number of antique varieties can be found in commerce if you are prepared to do some hunting, many countries are now forming national collections, and it is often possible to arrange to have grafting material from trees that interest you. Examples are the Brogdale Trust, Faversham, England, with huge collections in all top fruit species, and one devoted to peaches in the Tarn region of France. All these collections run tasting, grafting and other courses.

Opposite: This nineteenth-century painting from the Benary catalogue shows the mix of productive plants and decorative flowers that characterized the traditional kitchen garden.

Below: Decorative kitchen gardens always need vegetables with attractive foliage and stems. Ruby chard, shown here, is easy to grow, but look out also for exotic-leaved basils, spinaches, sorrels and brassicas.

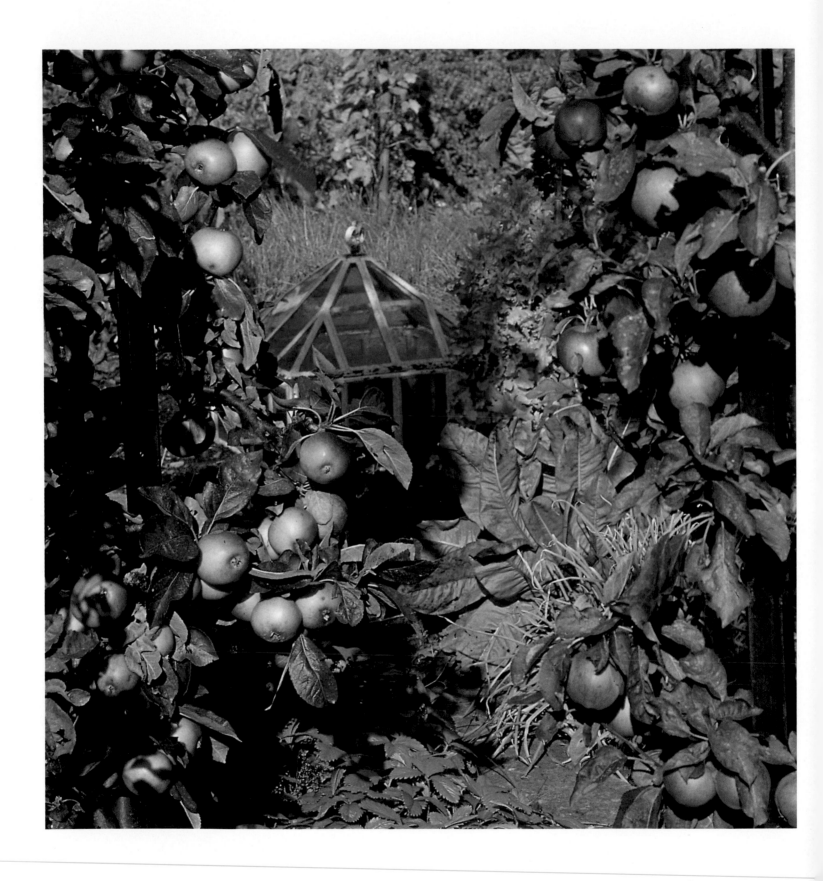

FRUIT TREES AND ORCHARD GARDENS

If your garden has space for a proper orchard, and you want to grow antique fruit trees, plant them as a quincunx, an arrangement of trees in use since ancient Greece and into modern times. The simplest layout had trees planted at the notional corners of a square, usually 4.5–7.5m (15–25ft) on the side, the grid generally running north/south and east/west, with the planting being as large as the owner had room for. A more complex and rather more interesting one had a fifth tree in the centre of each square.

If you can, give orchards some sort of enclosure. It was a moat and palisade in the grandest medieval examples, but a hedge of hawthorn or of mixed native trees and bushes, with simple hedgerow fruits, may be more practical for most contemporary gardeners. Inner paths were often hedged with gooseberry or common berberis (*Berberis vulgaris* is the only one to use, though not in the US, where upright forms of blueberry were often substituted). The trees themselves had an underplanting of grass, scattered with sweet violets, wild strawberries, spring bulbs and even an occasional rose bush (try *Rosa* 'Alba Maxima'). Seventeenth-century orchards often had their paths centred on a statue or an urn, or even a small summerhouse – still a perfect centrepiece. If you prefer informality and want to plant the orchard as wilderness, keep the trees at least 4.5m (15ft) apart and mow circulation paths between them.

In small gardens, just two or three trees will give great pleasure, but remember that for the best crop apples, pears, plums and hazels all need a suitable 'pollinator' combination of two different varieties. In tiny gardens, try espalier-pruned trees against the house or an outbuilding wall, or the single-stemmed cordons. Pruning does take time

in winter and high summer, but the results look good, and the crops can be heavy. If space is really limited, stick to apples and pears.

Malus APPLE

One of the most beautiful of all fruit trees, the apple probably originated in the Caucasus, as a hybrid between a number of local species of *Malus*. Primitive sorts can be found all over the region between Turkey and India. The Romans had many types, and orchards were extremely profitable. In Western Europe, apples gradually developed huge numbers of local varieties, many of which survived into the seventeenth century. Groups like the rennets, pippins, pearmains and russets are all from this date, though breeding within them has continued into this century. Many were in America by the seventeenth century and have given rise to hundreds of American varieties.

Good older apples include, from before 1600, 'Nonpareil', 'Golden Pippin', 'Calville Blanc' or 'Rouge d'Hiver'; 'Ribston Pippin' of about 1707; 'Ashmead's Kernel' from the late eighteenth century (a strong-growing tree with aromatic fruit); and 'Cox's Orange Pippin' from around 1830.

Mespilus MEDLAR

A native of Europe, the medlar was apparently ignored by the Romans, but every Renaissance writer knew it. By then there were many recipes for its use in the kitchen. Fruits were harvested when hard if they were to be kept into midwinter, or left on the tree until ripe (or 'bletted'). The tree has large flowers in spring, a picturesque shape and magnificent autumn colours. In the seventeenth century a free-standing tree or two might have been planted in the kitchen garden.

Opposite: Apples, including 'Devonshire Quarrenden' (from before 1700), pruned as single-stem cordons and supported by metal arches.

Above: 'Court Plat Pendu' probably dates from well before the sixteenth century. The fruits, small and russet yellow, make delicious winter eating.

Below: *Mespilus* 'Nottingham', with fruit like small, foreshortened pears in a fine amber brown. It has been known since the early eighteenth century and is probably older.

Above left: *Vitis* 'Black Hamburgh' is good on walls or trained up the inside of a conservatory. It fruits prolifically and has a delicious flavour.

Above centre: The gooseberry 'Whinham's Industry' shows how dark ripe fruits of some varieties can become; others ripen almost black. All make delicious dessert fruit.

Above right: Morellos are the only cherries that take easily to pruning; they can be trained as large fans and will fruit on a shady wall.

Prunus avium CHERRY

Sweet cherries originated in Greece or Turkey. After Lucullus carried some back to Rome in triumph, they spread rapidly through the Empire: the 'Kentish Red' (a type of morello cherry, sharp flavoured, but with a larger fruit) may date from Roman times. The variety called 'Noble', still available, was imported to Britain from Belgium by Tradescant the Elder. The earliest to crop is the pale 'May Duke', also seventeenth century. In eighteenth-and nineteenth-century orchards, trees were often underplanted with strawberries and currants; try that in yours. Edible cherries are as marvellous in flower as their decorative relatives.

Prunus domestica PLUM

Domesticated in Asia around 1000BC, long after the more refined damson, plums have been grown continuously since then. They reached America in the 1500s. Each continent has its own distinct varieties, with Chinese ones being especially distinctive. 'Coe's Golden Drop', from the late 1700s, is a delicious British one to grow. The most successful of all must be 'Victoria', now grown worldwide; it seems to have originated in 1840.

Prunus persica PEACH

Though called *Prunus persica*, the peach was first domesticated in China, where it was grown for its large pink flowers as well as the delicious fruit. It took many centuries to reach Europe; Pliny calls it 'recently introduced', but soon many sorts were grown all over the Roman empire. There were red- and white-skinned peaches in Europe in the early 1500s and the fruit reached America by 1565. There it became so common in some states that it was used to feed pigs or distilled to make brandy.

The varieties 'Rochester' and 'Peregrine' are both antique and delicious. But look for the 'Pêche de vigne', a variety coming true from seed, velvety yellow and succulent, and used in ancient and modern Italy as a prop for vines.

Pyrus PEAR

Originating in prehistoric western Asia, the pear was a 'fruit of the Gods' in Greece of 1000BC. The Romans had dozens of sorts, some for winter eating, and over 1,000 sorts exist today. For antique gardens, look for the delicious 'Jargonelle', 'Catillac' and 'Bergamotte' of 1600. The fruit of all three is small, with the first making late summer eating, the others not softening until winter, so store them carefully. Trees produce abundant crops, so pickled pears and chutneys are other good uses. There are also large numbers of extant nineteenth-century varieties.

Ribes x uva-crispa var. reclinatum GOOSEBERRY

A European native, used by both the Greeks and Romans. An ingredient of sauces in medieval Europe, new French sorts were being imported to Britain in the 1270s. Five hundred years later, there were so many enthusiastic growers that 'gooseberry clubs' sprang up and there were huge numbers of varieties. Sweet sorts remain most popular in Britain and North America, though sharp ones are essential in France and Germany, especially as sauces for fatty fish and meat.

Vitis VINE

Native to the eastern Mediterranean, vines were grown in the Middle East by 4000BC and there are Egyptian manuals on viticulture from 1,000 years later. Early Romans treated wine warily, but late Romans had vineyards all over the Empire, and wine and raisins were important commodities (Greek wines were best, and Pliny drank some that was 200 years old). Norman Britain had many vineyards, as did great estates 700 years later. Antiques can be very old: 'Muscat Frontignac' flourished in ancient Athens; the easy-to-grow 'Black Hamburgh' is probably sixteenth century. American settlers used native species, but soon began to hybridize these with European cultivars.

Above left: Peaches are easily trained against walls for early crops. Even in cold gardens with late springs they can fruit abundantly under glass.

Above centre: *Prunus* 'Coe's Drop': a delicious, juicy, eighteenth-century plum variety.

Above right: *Pyrus* 'William's Bon Chrétien' is a nineteenth-century representative of a group of autumn-ripening pears of which the earliest were grown in France in the sixteenth century.

THE VEGETABLE GARDEN

In the tiniest garden, where there is perhaps space for only a single fruit tree and a few rows of salads or vegetables, there is still room for something antique. For the tree, plant an old local variety of apple or peach, or a mulberry or medlar. Beneath it grow a row of skirret (*Sium sisarum*, with sweet parsnip-like roots), or of white Italian cucumbers and a pinch of antique radishes.

If you have more space, why not plant a potager? The combination of formal beds with vegetables and fruit can be quite as productive as the stolid rows of the conventional vegetable patch, and though proper crop rotation needs more planning than usual, a well-managed potager gives you somewhere pleasant to sit while you survey your growing crops. Providing there is room for an attractive formal arrangement of beds, there are endless visual possibilities to salads and vegetables. Try some of the red or tan-leafed chicories or lettuces, the scarlet midribs of ruby chard, the golden pods of some of the French beans, or the brilliantly coloured and edible flowers of borage, nasturtium and marigold.

For the more permanent parts of the design, make gooseberries, currants and all the tree fruits part of the decorative scheme, either by pruning them carefully into the desired shapes, or by planting them in big pots or tubs.

Below: Onions, with their many variations in the shape and skin colour of the bulbs, can make decorative as well as useful additions to the kitchen garden.

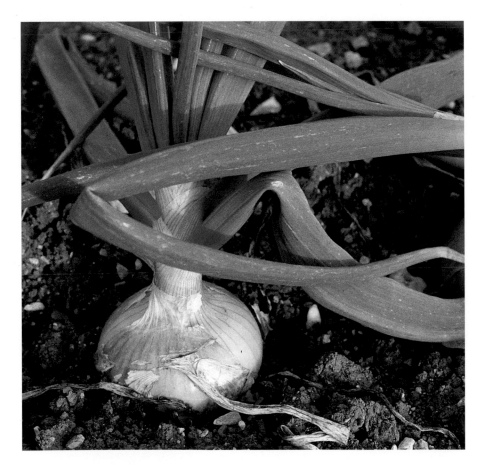

Allium cepa ONION

Probably grown in the earliest known gardens, in Mesopotamia, the onion was subsequently taken up by gardeners in ancient Egypt, Greece and Rome, and then given to the rest of the world. Oddly, Renaissance gardeners in Europe thought that it had all sorts of dangerous properties, and it wasn't even a cottage garden plant until the nineteenth century. There are huge numbers of varieties (hence the expression 'knowing your onions'), from the potato onions with their clusters of subterranean bulbs, and the Egyptian onion with groups of bulblets instead of flowers, to scallions (once used as an aphrodisiac), spring onions and more. The mild-flavoured and long-keeping 'Bedfordshire Champion' and silvery salad 'White Lisbon' are both early nineteenth century. The red-skinned 'Red Wethersfield' is an American of about the same date.

Welsh onions belong to a different species (*Allium fistulosum*), are ancient and have been gardened in Europe since at least 1629.

Allium porrum LEEK

Though leeks have been the badge of Wales since the Dark Ages, the earliest record dates from Egypt of 3000BC, and even in first-century Rome gourmets thought that the best ones came from there. The Emperor Nero imported them, thinking that they improved his voice. A much more various crop then than now, forms were once used for their foliage, others for side bulbs and offsets. The difference between leek varieties is not large, so even modern ones won't look out of place in antique gardens. The heavy-cropping and very hardy 'Musselburgh' dates from around 1834, and was grown in America soon after.

Amaranthus AMARANTHUS

A popular North American crop; many species give edible foliage and seeds. *Amaranthus hypochondriacus* can have remarkably decorative foliage; the golden-leafed form is a handsome addition to the potager. But there are maroon, scarlet and speckled variants, yielding brilliant dyes used by Native Americans; the leaves can also be steamed in the manner of spinach. Both this and *A. leucocarpus* are important grain crops.

Though amaranthuses reached Europe by the late sixteenth century, they have not really strayed much outside the flower garden, where forms like 'Prince's Feather' were much liked.

Above: *Amaranthus hypochondriacus* is a spectacular plant even in its basic form, but there are still more dramatic varieties with scarlet and golden foliage.

Left: Leeks, winter hardy and cropped throughout that season, give welcome structural emphasis to the kitchen garden when most of the ground is bare.

Above left: Fennel soon makes large perennial plants which can be used to give scale to the kitchen plot, as well as flavour to salads and baked fish.

Below left: Artichokes, with their handsome foliage, are essential in the antique potager.

Below right: Savoy cabbages, hardy in all but the coldest gardens, are delicious and decorative.

Brassica CABBAGE

A huge group, probably domesticated in Asia Minor. The Greeks had a kale by 600BC, and the Romans grew a head-forming cabbage which they thought bad for their eyesight. Red cabbages were grown in Germany by 1150, and three sorts of savoy were known by the sixteenth century. Many sorts have vanished, including the ancient 'musk cabbage'. One early variety, 'Couve Tronchuda', with its open growth and fleshy pale midribs, is still used to make a special soup in Portugal. It tastes best after heavy frosting. Other survivors include 'Early Jersey Wakefield' sorts of around 1880 (grown in American gardens by 1885). 'Dwarf Green Curled' savoy and 'Winningstadt', a good variety for salads, are both of 1859; and 'Wheelers Imperial', with its solid cones of grey-green foliage, is from 1849. Perhaps the oldest is 'Premium Late Flat Dutch', which dates from before 1700.

Cucurbita PUMPKIN, SQUASH

This is an American crop, covering several species of the genus. All were probably domesticated between 10,000 and 6000BC, perhaps originally for the seeds, roasted as they are today in the Middle East, rather than for the delicious flesh of the fruit. The marrows are most familiar in Europe, whether harvested young as courgettes or left to mature. They crop in cooler climates than many pumpkins; antiques include 'Vegetable Marrow' and 'Boston Marrow'. Pumpkins and squashes are both better to eat and to look at.

As the marvellous fruit store well, they must have reached Europe very soon after Columbus landed, and spread around the Mediterranean region soon after. They may have reached northern Europe from Turkey, hence the name 'Turk's Cap' ('Turk's Turban' in America, where there seems to be no native name) some time in the sixteenth century. Antique varieties such as 'Green Striped Cushaw' and 'Chestnut', common in America, are still unusual in Europe, though modern variants are becoming more familiar.

Cynara ARTICHOKE

The artichoke was admired by the ancient Greeks. In Rome, Pliny the Elder found that it was the most expensive vegetable in the markets, with crops being imported from as far afield as North Africa. In medieval Europe, it was vastly popular and thought to be aphrodisiac. American gardens had artichokes by the sixteenth century. Plants grown from modern seed will cover the entire range of variation; alternatively, in both America and Europe, look for 'Green Globe' of 1828. Its big scales are not too heavily spined, and have large quantities of flesh at their bases.

Foeniculum FENNEL

Fennel has been cultivated since earliest times and Roman cooks had several forms from which to choose: 'sweet' fennel in many variants (there were special sorts to provide roots, leaf 'bulbs', stems and foliage), as well as 'bitter' fennel (used principally to flavour alcohol).

Of the 'sweet' fennels, some root varieties still available in Italy have roots tender all the way through like parsnips and are delicious. Particularly in the south, forms are also grown with juicy stems reluctant to become woody which are sliced into salads. 'Zefa Fino', grown in America since 1890, is an old 'Florence' fennel, a form in which the lowest parts of the leaf stalks are succulent and wrap around one another to make a sort of bulb. Of the herb (bitter) fennels, try the fine one with purple-bronze foliage and stems.

Above: 'Turk's Turban' pumpkins have wildly decorative fruits which last well when harvested. The deep orange flesh is richly flavoured and delicious baked.

Above left: Spinach can be used to give quick rows of greenery to fill in spaces left by the harvesting of other crops. Some forms have decorative 'savoyed' or frilled leaves.

Above right: The runner bean 'Painted Lady' (of the early seventeenth century) makes a handsome climber and crops heavily too.

Right: The wild tomato is not too distant from the 'Gardener's Delight' shown here, which looks delightful scrambling over an arbour or up a tripod of poles in a warm garden.

Opposite: The pea 'Kelvedon Wonder' is a form of one of the most ancient garden crops.

Lycopersicon TOMATO

Strictly a fruit, tomatoes are included here because of their widespread use in salads and savoury dishes. Probably first seen by Europeans in Mexico in the sixteenth century, they were thought to be poisonous. Why what was so obviously a crop plant for the Native Americans should be regarded as poisonous in Europe is not clear, though the flower and fruit do resemble a number of very poisonous European members of the family.

In Europe, tomatoes first entered the kitchen in Italy, and the habit soon reached around the Mediterranean. They were rarely eaten in cautious northern Europe until the nineteenth and even early twentieth century.

Early introductions included red, yellow and white forms, with the red in two varieties: small and round, and large, flat and lobed. This last sort was thought to have the best flavour (it still has) and is nowadays referred to as part of the 'Marmande' group – the one seen most commonly in French country markets. Many sorts of cherry tomato were in widespread cultivation in Central America by the time of the Spanish invasion.

Phaseolus BEAN

From Central and South America – excavations in Mexico show that they have been grown for at least 2,000 years – runner beans (*Phaseolus coccineus*) were in European gardens probably early in the sixteenth century, though Tradescant the Elder is sometimes credited with their introduction. For a century or two they were grown only for their brilliant red flowers, twined up arbours and over walls. They first appeared on the table in the mid-eighteenth century, when a botanist named Philip Miller discovered how delicious they were. Old sorts include the 'Painted Lady' of 1633. I grow it up bamboo tripods amongst the cabbages.

French or kidney beans (*Phaseolus vulgaris*) are also ancient. Radio carbon dates of 8000BC have been obtained at archaeological sites in Peru, and they were certainly cultivated in North America by 5000BC. They reached Europe in the early sixteenth century. They were most popular in Italy, hence the early English and French names of 'Roman' beans. There do not seem to have been many varieties available, though by the early eighteenth century there were climbers as well as a few bush types. That soon changed, and by the 1880s vast numbers had come into commerce. Spectacular pod types can be found, some nearly 60cm (2ft) in length, others coloured violet, yellow or scarlet, plain or streaked. There are also many variations in seed design and decoration; variations in flavour do exist, but are less marked.

Pisum PEAS

The sorts of peas now used for drying have been found in excavations of 7000BC, making them as old as wheat and barley. They were in Western Europe before the Roman expansion, though the Romans themselves had no clearly defined sorts.

Sugar-snap peas were grown in sixteenth-century gardens, and by the eighteenth century there were huge numbers of now-lost varieties of podded peas – lovely-sounding ones too, with names like rose, rouncival, sickle, tufted and Hotspur peas. In that century, much development had taken place in sweet-seeded varieties that are most suitable for eating fresh: 'Lincoln' is from 1849, and the American 'Tall Telephone' from 1878. Some others maintained by gardeners are far more ancient but not in commerce.

Spinacia SPINACH

A native plant of south-western Asia, spinach was introduced to Britain, possibly from Spain, in the sixteenth century. It seems not to have been used by the Greeks or Romans, but was known to medieval Arab physicians. It was also used in fireworks (paper soaked in spinach juice acts as touchpaper). Savoy-leafed, prickly and smooth-seeded sorts are all antique. Try 'Bloomsdale Long Standing' for the first (though it is only just an antique for American gardens), and 'Giant Thick Leaved Prickly' for the second.

KITCHEN HERBS

Though the idea of a herb garden is immensely attractive, in the real garden most of the useful culinary herbs, especially the mints, tarragon, oreganos and thymes, are not especially exciting plants to look at, and the mints, in particular, can colonize the ground in ways that make them a menace. Give the herb garden a strong form, using broad pathways (most herbs sprawl) and formal elements, perhaps clipped rosemary or bay. Antique gardens used some of the smaller and more polite herbs to edge paths and beds. Chives, parsley and some of the tougher thymes can look excellent like this, though unless you have an unusually large household, they will produce far more of a crop than you can possibly use.

Very aromatic herbs, like rosemary, lavender, bay and half-herbs like lemon verbena, should, anyway, be grown near wherever you are going to sit in the garden. Some gardeners also choose to plant the smaller thymes among the paving stones of that area, but beware of them if you like going barefoot on a summer's day; thyme flowers attract bees in quantity.

The mints, of which there are huge numbers, though only one or two that are necessary for the kitchen, are best grown in large containers – in my garden ginger mint makes spectacular pots. Tarragon is best grown in some out-of-the-way spot (where you can put the horseradish too) where its untidy growth will not be a nuisance. Most of the others are far better simply integrated into the vegetable garden, though the marjorams can happily be planted among the flowers in the cottage border. If your garden is cool, basil is best grown indoors in a pot, where it can look (and smell) extremely good.

Allium CHIVES

Native from Britain to China and even North America, chives were probably gathered from the wild until the sixteenth century. By the eighteenth, they were used as a crisp edging for beds in the kitchen garden, where they look excellent, especially when their tiny globes of pale mauve flowers are in full show. There are no named varieties, though there is a rare, and probably antique, form with white flowers. Take the shears to them when the flowers fade, or you will have huge numbers of seedlings.

Above: Dill, an annual, looks like a small fennel but has a very different and distinctive flavour, essential in many dishes, especially ones from the Northern European cuisine.

Coriandrum CORIANDER

Popular in the kitchens of ancient Rome, coriander may have been domesticated from wild plants in Asia Minor. Seed was purchased for Hampton Court in 1567, and the herb was grown in fields in Norfolk in the eighteenth century. Dried crystallized seedpods were used to perfume the breath and to aid digestion. In the kitchen, seeds were added to the basting fluids for roast meats. Grow a row or two amongst the vegetables.

Mentha MINT

All the mints have been widely used since ancient times, probably more for real or supposed medicinal properties than in the kitchen. Pennyroyal was the most admired, being used to dampen hysteria, speed the menopause and disperse fleas and flies. Spearmint, used for sauces on lamb and as a flavouring for pea soup since earliest times, was thought the most useful by Pliny. He said that it was good for the memory, acted as a vermifuge and stopped milk curdling in the hot Roman summer. The Romans also rubbed peppermint on their tables before a meal, perhaps to ensure good digestion, as well as to preserve a fresh smell.

Ocimum BASIL

Originating in tropical Asia and Africa, basil is a plant of great mystery. Its full name of 'basilikum' means king. It may have been associated with kingship, for there were taboos surrounding it, evidenced by an association with snakes, worms, scorpions, maggots, headaches and blindness. Perhaps it was thought safe for only kings to handle. Even by 200BC, the ancient Greeks thought it hurtful for stomach, eyes and wits. Other ancient beliefs suggested that if powdered basil was put under a stone, it bred serpents. Seed, it was said, should be sown with curses.

Anethum DILL

Dill was much used all over Europe in Renaissance medicines, especially for curing flatulence, various female ailments and also as an aphrodisiac, though too much of it was thought to impair the eyesight. Dill is essential in every kitchen garden, used particularly in marinades for salmon and other grand fish, to flavour pickled cucumbers, and for sauces. It can also be found as an ingredient in a surprising number of perfumes.

Left: The pinky-purple young flowers of coriander look good if the plants are sown as rows between rows of 'January King' cabbage, or between leeks or red-leafed cabbages.

Below left: Some of the mints – this one the variegated apple mint, admired by connoisseurs of both kitchen and garden – are very decorative. Try ginger mint, too.

Below centre: *Mentha spicata*, like all its relatives, spreads wildly, so grow it in tubs or old buckets sunk to ground level. To dry, harvest the stems before flowering begins.

Below right: Seedling basil plants are used at this size by Italian cooks for pesto sauce. It's worth sowing a pinch of seed regularly through the summer.

Whatever its disadvantages, by the eighteenth century it was widely used in salads and ragouts. The herb includes types with purple, frilled or savoyed leaves. The purple 'Red Rubin' is similar to ancient forms, and there is also a red form of the sacred 'Tulsi' basil (*Ocimum tenuiflorum*). Grow the ancient bush basil (*Ocimum minimum*) and you will have neat domes of greenery which flower as summer ends. The flavour is as good as that of the more familiar culinary varieties.

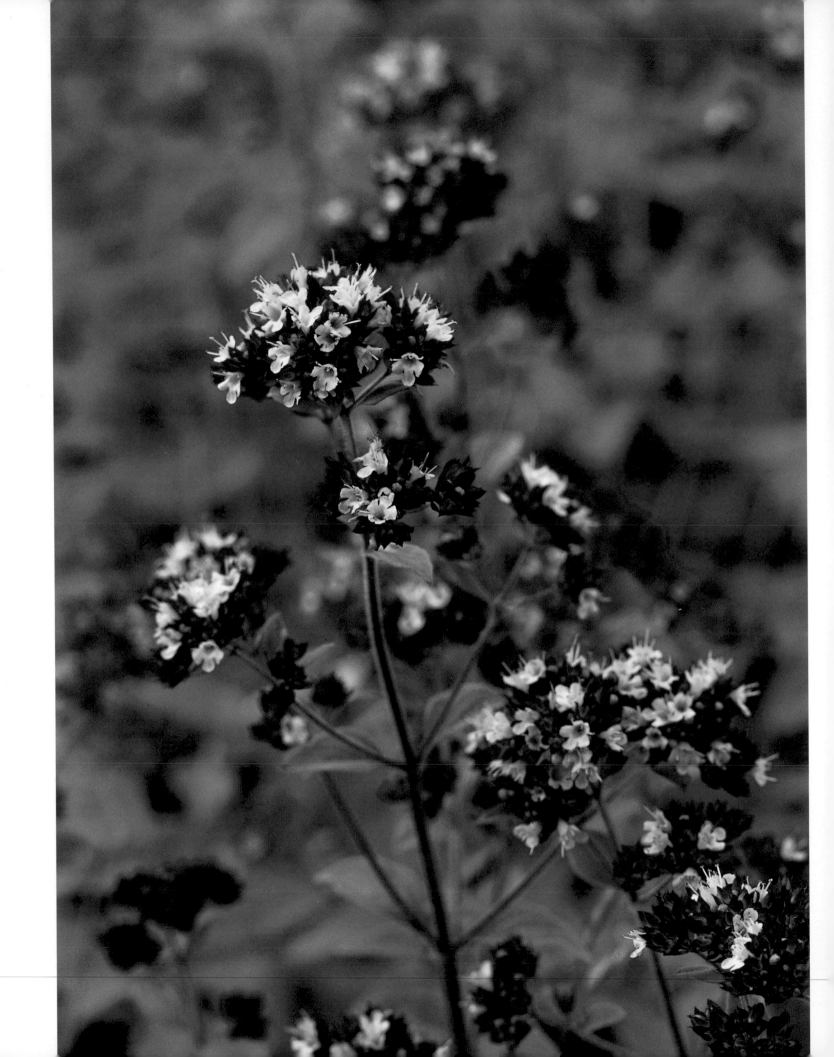

Origanum MARJORAM

Marjoram is often said to be a mid-sixteenth century introduction to the garden, but by then it had such huge numbers of medicinal as well as culinary uses that it must be very much older. Its oil has been used to stop toothache, to loosen stiff joints, perfume the hair and as a face powder, as well as for snuff and ragouts. The flowering tops of the plant, which has a more interesting savour than the purely leafy parts, were once used to dye woollen cloth a purple colour and linens a reddish brown. In the eighteenth century, many garden variants were grown, with crisped, frilled or variegated leaves. Of the latter, 'Gold Tipped' is the most attractive. Many are vigorous and need clipping to keep them in order. Use different sorts to create pretty knot gardens, or leave clumps to flower and attract every bee for miles.

Petroselinum PARSLEY

Parsley is the most widely grown herb, and has been since at least the end of the seventeenth century. It must have been introduced by the Romans, who used it as a flavouring and in medicines. They grew both flat and curly kinds (the flat sort is still widely used on the Continent and has a slightly lighter and sharper flavour). Perhaps because the flat sort was more easily mistaken for one of the poisonous umbellifers, it was used at funerals – Pliny said that the Sardinian parsley was poisonous. Even in the sixteenth century, parsley was sometimes accused of causing epilepsy. Stalks of flat-leafed parsley, sometimes sold as 'French parsley', can be blanched like celery to make a pleasant vegetable, and it has a much better taste, green, in salads than curled-leaf parsley. 'Hamburg parsley' is a variant grown for the swollen root, and was eaten as winter fare by the late seventeenth century.

Thymus THYME

A herb comprising several species and many hybrids, all part of a huge and complex genus. Most of the highly aromatic species are native to Mediterranean countries. In ancient Greece, thyme was thought to give courage and revive the spirits. Thyme honey was then, and still is, much admired. The Romans made extensive use of thyme as a medicine, much of it surviving into the nineteenth century, including treatments for melancholia, epilepsy, hangovers, toothache and insomnia.

In the kitchen, it was also used as a flavouring for roasts and stews, and even to flavour sheep on the hoof; thyme-fed lamb was an expensive delicacy. Renaissance gardeners liked to plant borders of thyme around kitchen garden paths, while their eighteenth-century counterparts bordered flowerbeds with both gold- and silver-leafed varieties (*Thymus* × *citriodorus* 'Aurea' and *T.* × *citriodorus* 'Argentea' respectively).

Opposite: Marjoram, essential for the kitchen, is easy to grow from seed and perennial thereafter. A vigorous sub-shrub, its late summer flowers attract bees and butterflies.

Above left: Thymes come in a wide range of shapes, sizes and savours. This is one of the large-leafed culinary sorts.

Above right: Curly-leafed parsley remains a good decorative and medicinal plant, even though many gastronomes now prefer the flat-leafed variety.

A PRODUCTIVE POTAGER

Above: Apples trained on arches and a formal layout based on a design of 1618 make a perfect back garden for a village house like this one.

Right: A glass and iron cloche for forcing salads and young vegetables makes a pretty addition to the scene.

This village kitchen garden not only contains many ancient varieties of vegetable, herb and fruit, it even has a ground plan based on an antique design. One of the woodcuts in William Lawson's *A New Orchard and Garden*, a delightful book written in 1618, shows a plan for just such a walled garden, with diagonal cross walks and a central bed. Lawson is so eloquent on his subject that, having read his book, it is hard to plant anything as unproductive as a flower.

Modern gardeners might not care for Lawson's suggestion of statuary or consorts of viols among their cabbages, but we can surely not disagree with him when he writes, 'Whereas every other pleasure commonly fills some one of our senses, and that only with delight; this [the kitchen garden] makes all our senses swim in pleasure, and that with infinite variety.... View now with delight the works of your own hands, your fruit trees of all sorts, loaden with sweet blossoms, and fruits of all tastes, operations, and colours: your trees standing in comely order, which way soever you look... your borders on every side hanging, and dropping with Feberries, Raspberries, Barberries, Currans, and the roots of your trees powdered with Strawberries, Red, White, and Green, what a pleasure this is!' Indeed.

The bones of this decorative kitchen garden were laid down in 1987, and though it looks large, it is only 10m (about 30ft) square. It has the benefit of a sunny, south-facing site, which is more or less level (though kitchen gardens like this can be adapted for terraced plots), and one which also has a little shelter from other parts of the garden and from adjoining cottages, though even with that

Above: Modern ruby chard looks no different to antique sorts (see page 113), so is perfectly acceptable in an antique kitchen garden.

Left: Lettuces and leeks are allowed to run to seed to show the additional beauty of kitchen garden crops.

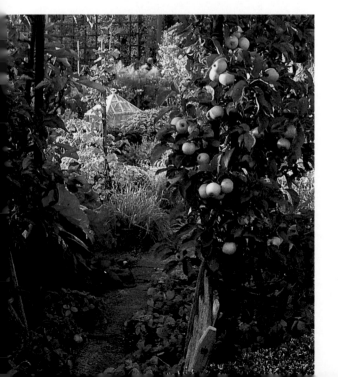

the owners have found that standard-pruned currants have been beheaded by the wind. The soil is a good heavy loam.

The garden's form is given by the outer framework of box hedging, allowed to grow 45cm (1ft 6in) high and deep. The paths of concrete slabs are edged with thick growth of Welsh onions and chives. The circular central bed, devoted to herbs, is edged with rope-moulded Victorian garden tiles. Each of the entrances into the garden has been given a handsome and sturdy metal arch, large enough and deep enough to support cordons of old varieties of apple and pear.

Each arch has four cordons of fruit on either side, allowing a good range of old varieties to be grown in a relatively small space. Among the delights featured here are, of apples, 'American Mother', 'Devonshire Quarrenden', 'Ellison's Orange' and 'St Edmund's Russet'; and of pears 'Beure Superfin', 'Glow Red William' and the tiny but delicious 'Jargonelle'. Though the winter and summer pruning is time-consuming, the pleasure of having that range of smells, colours and tastes is, as Lawson wrote, a considerable compensation.

Alpine strawberries are used to cover the ground beneath the trees, something else that William Lawson suggested. For more height within the garden, wirework frames and obelisks are used to support runner and climbing French beans. As the vegetation of these is cleared away after the first frosts, the obelisks give winter structure of their own. The other garden 'props' help winter too, though many are also functional. The modern seakale pots are used for blanching the emerging shoots of seakale, a delicious and perennial

Opposite above: A globe artichoke in full flower; harvest before the flower opens if you want to eat the buds.

Opposite below: Evening light on the potager. The cloches date from between 1820 and 1860, but attractive modern copies are easy to find.

relative of the cabbage, popular at table since the eighteenth century. Except where there are perennial vegetables such as artichokes, seakale and asparagus, the vegetable beds are redesigned and replanted every season. Perennial vegetables are left in permanent rows. As the garden is planned to give salads, vegetables and herbs as early and late in the season as possible, the pretty Victorian cloches, forcing pots and bell jars are in active use. The garden produces far more than the owners need and the unused lettuces, chicories and beets are left to show the potential of their flowers and seedheads. To stop the box hedging taking too much nourishment from the soil, it is root-pruned every season or so by using a spade to slice downwards along the length of the hedges.

All potagers are helped by a little colour from flowers as well as that from vegetable and salad foliage. Here, the flowers are all edible ones. Borage and marigold are both antiques, though this garden uses the late-Victorian variegated form of the ancient nasturtium. The unusual herbs and vegetables include the variegated land-cress (*Barbarea verna* 'Variegata'), popular in Victorian bedding schemes, though it also makes good eating; 'Ragged Jack' kale; the delightful pink and white runner bean 'Painted Lady'; the blue-podded pea, and a fascinating and rare red-leafed sorrel I've not come across before, with large spear-shaped leaves in a fine mahogany red. This is certainly a plant with a past and even more certainly one with a future.

Above left and centre: Box hedges frame the design, and wild strawberries (*Fragaria vesca*) edge the paths. The centre of the garden is marked by a grand terracotta pot, which is eventually to contain a topiary bay tree.

Above right: The wild European strawberry produces runners, though these are easily controlled.

THE CONTAINER GARDEN

Plants have been grown in pots for three thousand years, and today almost every gardener still makes use of at least a few plants in containers. In ancient China of 1000BC, pot plants were domestically important, expensive and commonly given elegant containers. In the courtyard houses of ancient Greece, pot plants were used for decoration, though they were also functional: at the Hephaisteion in the Agora of Athens, a row of unidentified trees was planted in large pots and sunk in cuttings in the rock to make an avenue.

Roman horticulture, too, made extensive use of containers, not only for citrus fruits and vines, but also to help with forcing cherries and figs (slaves had to move the pots around to keep them in the sun against a warm wall). Potted fruit trees were carried into the dining space when the fruit was ripe. Wall paintings show that decorative containers were also used for roses, pomegranates and oleanders, and we know that plants were transported around the Empire in pots.

Left: Lilies, topiary box, Paris daisies and tiny oranges are all part of this assemblage of containers in a city garden.
Above: Potted auriculas in an enchanting painting of 1817, by Pancrace Bessa.

In the Middle East at the same time, garden pots were used in the Roman manner for planting out such things as lemons and vines, and numbers have been found at the winter palaces of Herod Tulu Abu el-Alayik, south of Jericho. Farther west, similar pots have also been discovered at the Roman excavations at Watling Street in the City of London.

Grand medieval gardeners continued the Roman use of pots (large numbers of earthenware pots were ordered for Hampton Court in 1515); poorer ones used containers of wattle or crude earthenware, and had them on windowsills, by the well or (sometimes planted with fragrant carnations or pinks) next to turf seats. Once excavations of ancient Rome began during the Renaissance, Italian grandees copied Roman models (often funerary urns) and grew elegant potfuls of pomegranates, lemons or bitter oranges, to decorate their loggias, staircases and grand entrance halls.

In prosperous late-medieval gardens, at least in southern Europe, there was often a 'winter house' where valuable potted plants were kept during that season. As it had a fireplace, lemons and oranges managed to survive both cold and dark until late spring. Most citruses coped well, even when the only thermometer was a saucer filled with water – when it froze, fires were lit. Throughout Europe, big collections of varieties were kept and maintained as being appropriate to the gardens of the wealthy. By the thirteenth century, the Chiaramontesi garden in northern Italy had several thousand lemons and oranges. In Renaissance mansions, conditions for overwintering oleanders, myrtles and pomegranates and brand-new American exotics such as agaves and opuntias were at least slightly better, for the handsome and well-lit pavilions used for the owners' summer banquets were often transformed into the winter quarters for exotic 'greens'.

Once glass became cheaper, a century or so later, it could be used for almost any garden building: summerhouses, plant houses and primitive orangeries, which had just begun to appear in the late sixteenth century, became common throughout Europe in the 1600s. Container gardening soon became an important skill. In a few decades, tender plants from all over the world were grown, still often outdoors during the summer, and overwintered under glass.

By the beginning of the nineteenth century, cast-iron technology (part of the foundation of the Industrial Revolution) had improved so much that log-burning stoves, heating pipes and even the greenhouses themselves could be manufactured easily and cheaply. Soon, the rich had plant houses that could duplicate the most tropic climes and that they could fill with orchids, bromeliads, ferns, palms and other exotics from anywhere in the world. Only a few decades later, even middle-class houses had conservatories in which the owners could cultivate rare plants bought in the imported plant auctions that took place in almost every major city in Europe. The Industrial Revolution also made plant containers themselves cheaper, and soon every house and garden in Europe and America had at least a few geraniums or ivies in a tin or cast-iron or terracotta urn.

Above: The delicious and early-fruiting 'May Duke' cherry.

Opposite: The interior of a Victorian vine house; the bed of soil at floor level would have been used for forcing early vegetables, or even for growing pineapples. The vines were planted with their roots outside. Heating was probably provided by chimney flues running up the back wall.

GARDENING WITH CONTAINERS

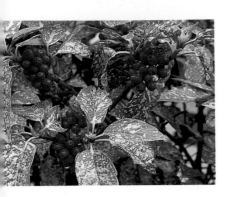

Above: The berries and variegated foliage of *Aucuba japonica*, a popular plant in nineteenth-century inner-city gardens.

Below: Aucubas are easy to grow from cuttings if you want to copy this amusing arrangement of pots.

Good places for pots in cottage gardens include by doorways, on low walls, around a sundial or in clusters by seats. In topiary gardens and if you have large ones, pots can frame a view or even make its termination. In the kitchen garden, they can mark the junction of paths or the centre of beds, or stand beside the bean arbour. They make good homes for invasive herbs like mint or floppy ones like marjoram. The rose garden, sometimes difficult to structure and often a trifle flat once the main flowering season is over, can usefully be decorated with all sorts of containers, either for topiary to give strong architectural emphasis, or for sumptuous flowering plants to give colour until autumn. Under glass, containers should be a movable feast.

In gardens for antique plants, it is worth planting in classic types of container. Terracotta garden pots are widely available, from tiny to huge. These pots look splendid and soon appear suitably aged. Plants grow well in them and are easily repotted except when the pots are enormous. The pots can be had variously decorated; swags of foliage and satyrs' masks are the most traditional.

'Versailles' tubs, cube-shaped with decorative finials, and handles for mobility, look equally good with topiary, standard trees (they were used at Versailles for an ancient collection of citrus trees, purchased for Louis XIV) or a tumble of agapanthus. Although they are commonly painted dark green, some old Italian gardens have the framework in grey and the panels in olive.

When choosing a container, consider first whether it is to stand outdoors all year and, if so, what your winters are like. While some terracottas can stand reasonable amounts of frost, serious cold will flake off the rims or crack them apart. Wintered indoors (even in an outhouse) they survive perfectly well.

Plastics are winterproof but weather badly, becoming dirty rather than attractively patinated. Glass fibre does better, and the better imitation Versailles tubs and painted or metal urns make good 'focal points' outdoors all year round. Metal containers need some care; if the soil inside gets waterlogged, then freezes, cast iron can split.

Any of the plants mentioned in this book can look handsome in a container. Experiment. Fill pots with bulbs: many lilies fare better in pots than in the open border (*Lilium tigrinum* does wonderfully, though try the nineteenth-century *L. longiflorum* too). Many annuals also do well: try big pots of *Nicotiana affinis* or *N. sylvestris*, or smaller ones of Chinese annual dianthuses.

The following are some plants not covered elsewhere in the book that thrive in containers. Some are essentially hardy in northern gardens, but can be moved under cover in harsh conditions. Others are more or less tender, depending on your climate. With tough winters, even plants like the species of *Agapanthus*, particularly forms of *A. africanus* (early nineteenth century), need to be under glass, and in northern gardens, ancient pot plants like the oleanders barely have enough summer sun to make them flower. There, too, most citrus plants need to be under glass all year, though some, like the gorgeous 'Imperial' lemon, will appreciate a month or two outdoors to produce flower buds. *Canna indica* (look for the

eighteenth-century plant with variegated leaves) can cope, but northern winds batter the flowers, making shelter essential. Fuchsias have some species that are hardy in the north, but many antique hybrids need to be indoors for most of the year. Rhododendrons, too, have marvellous antiques (try 'Lady Alice Fitzwilliam' and 'Princess Alice') that need to be in pots, though the perfume is so good you won't mind looking after them.

Above: The calamondin (*Citronella microcarpa*) is easy to grow in a bright, frost-free place, and its flowers smell just as good as those of lemons and grapefruit. The smallish 'oranges' can be used like kumquats.

Acer MAPLE

Small yards can often be heavily shaded, but they are also sheltered. If you need interesting foliage and powerful autumn colours, then try some of the myriad varieties of Japanese maple (*Acer palmatum*). These were immensely popular in Japan and are found painted on medieval screens, though their greatest popularity was in the seventeenth and eighteenth centuries – the first Japanese book about them was published in six volumes in 1710. Choice varieties began to appear in the West from around 1820; few remain, but try 'Osakazuki' from around 1840 or the smaller and purple-leafed 'Umegae' from a few decades later. Providing they don't dry out, they make fascinating plants for large pots or tubs.

Right: The small maples, especially forms of *Acer palmatum*, look splendid in pots and especially suit small, sheltered, formal spaces. All of them colour brilliantly in autumn.

Below: Paris daisies, this one the basic species, are easily clipped into shape early in the season and then left to flower for the rest of the summer.

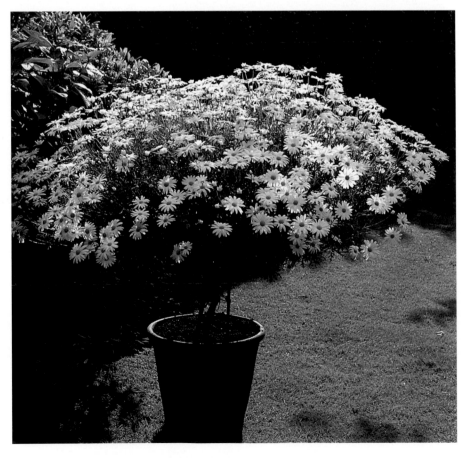

Argyranthemum PARIS DAISY

Argyranthemum frutescens, in its simplest yellow-flowered form, was introduced to Britain from Paris in the late seventeenth century, hence its common name, though the basic species is native to the Far East. Other variants soon arrived. The oldest sorts, with single white flowers and jagged olive-green foliage, make marvellous plants for large tubs or vast earthenware pots. Clip into domes when they become messy.

Brugmansia suaveolens DATURA

This species has marvellous pendant white flowers, sometimes almost 30cm (12in) long, heavy with perfume at night. From Central America, it was in eighteenth-century European glasshouses; the gorgeous double white *Brugmansia × candida* may have been grown since the seventeenth century. The annual *B. meteloides*, a sprawling bush if well fed, has enormous white and perfumed flowers, making it a good subsitute if you have nowhere to overwinter the other species.

Crinum CRINUM

The largest and handsomest of the antique bulbs is the dramatic 'sea lily' (*Crinum bulbispermum*). Brought to Europe from South Africa probably in the late seventeenth century, it makes luxuriant clumps of large leaves, from which arise stems up to 1.5m (5ft) tall, topped with large flowers, which are white or sometimes striped in pinkish purple. The more recent (nineteenth-century) hybrid *C. × powellii* is a strong candy pink. The perfume of both is delicious and heady, and especially strong on warm summer evenings.

Thought to be tender when first introduced, crinums were often grown under glass all year, when several crops of flowers were obtained. Dry plants off in winter.

Dendranthema CHRYSANTHEMUM

Though there are well over thirty Asian species, the decorative chrysanthemums (complicated hybrids involving *Chrysanthemum indicum* and others) probably originated in China long before 500BC. They were exported to Japan about 800AD, and to Holland in the late seventeenth century. The first ones to arrive in Europe were lost, but others reached Britain in 1790, causing great excitement. Between 1816 and 1823, seventeen new sorts were added, and experiments in crossing soon began. Growers produced some incredible plants: one, in a 40cm (16in) pot, won all the prizes; it was said to be over 8m (27ft) in circumference and to have carried over 1,000 flowers. The Chinese would have been horrified to hear this; they allowed their plants no more than four or five perfect blooms.

Few old cultivars have survived intact with their names. 'Emperor of China' is one, and may be one of the ancient Chinese garden plants. But antique groups, rather than original varieties, can be

Above: Pink and powerfully fragrant, this is *Crinum x powellii*, a nineteenth-century hybrid of the old seventeenth-century 'sea lily'.

Left: *Chrysanthemum* (now *Dendranthema*) 'Quill Elegance'. Quilled flowers like this had been developed for showing by the 1830s.

identified. Old Chinese forms had masses of incurving petals, to give a globe or a bun-shaped bloom. Old Japanese sorts had recurved petals, giving a shaggier bloom. Of European developments, there were no pom-pom types before 1846, no anemone-types before 1856 and no varieties with heavily reflexed petals before 1862.

Dendrobium ORCHID

Once large numbers of gardeners in northern Europe and North America had greenhouses and conservatories, the jungles of Asia and Central and South America were soon ransacked for beautiful plants to put in them. At first, though, the tropical warmth and humidity necessary to grow orchids were the preserve of the very rich. As early as 1839, the ducal glasshouses at Chatsworth House in Derbyshire were packed with orchids, many collected specifically for the Duke of Devonshire. In that year, a plate was published of His Grace's *Dendrobium paxtonii*, the most magnificent orchid then in cultivation. It had only just flowered, the immense plant having been shipped whole from the Amazon. If you want to seek it out, it can be found in some garden centres.

By 1852, there were auctions in London of Guatemalan orchids, and other genera of orchid such as *Vanda* and *Cymbidium* were becoming more widely grown. What I consider the most gorgeous of all the vandas (*V. rothschildianum*) is an antique, and although it is a delicate mauve, other vandas come close to that rarest of garden colours, a genuine blue, and some have purple or mottled foliage.

Some *Dendrobium* species, including *D. nobile*, were grown by the 1820s. Many are easy to grow and reflower. In northern Europe, dendrobiums and some cymbidiums can be grown outdoors in shade during the summer, and brought indoors in September. Many will flower soon thereafter.

Although some orchids need surprisingly dry conditions, many still do best if you can re-create the lush surroundings of their native tropics. These will benefit from a daily mist-spraying, but the compost should never be allowed to get sodden.

Heliotropium HELIOTROPE

Though they are happy outside during the summer months, heliotropes can be kept in flower until early winter under glass, where the smell is delicious. They reached their greatest perfection and variety in Victorian gardens in summer, and in their conservatories in winter. Heliotropes are essential to any garden of the period.

Most varieties are hybrids between species of *Heliotropium* that arrived from Peru in the 1750s. They made little headway until the second decade of the nineteenth century, when Regency gardeners had good orangeries and glasshouses. The modern named forms, from deep purple through palest mauve to pure white, are all comparable to their nineteenth-century ancestors and may be identical.

Opposite, above and below: Gorgeous hybrid cymbidiums like these were soon developed from species being imported to Europe in the early nineteenth century.

Left: The sumptuous *Vanda rothschildiana* was named in the mid-1800s after that orchid-loving dynasty.

Above: Seedlings of the 'Marine' strain of heliotrope can give deep purple plants. One this size should perfume a small patio.

Above left: *Pelargonium* 'Miss Burdett Coutts' shows how colourful even the leaves of some nineteenth-century varieties could be; the flower buds were often pinched out.

Above right: Pungently lemon-scented *Pelargonium crispum minor* grows luxuriantly outdoors in a big pot, but is as happy in a small one on the windowsill.

Hydrangea HYDRANGEA

A large genus of shrubs and a few climbers, with species growing in Asia and North America. The American *Hydrangea arborescens* makes a wonderful tub plant at Hidcote Manor in Gloucestershire, and in any garden will have flower trusses in good condition until the late autumn. It was introduced to Europe in 1736. The following decades saw many more arrivals, mostly from China and Japan. There, many varieties were ancient garden plants, but in Europe breeding began only at the end of the nineteenth century. The plant called *Hydrangea* 'Joseph Banks', with its vast heads of greeny-cream flowers, later pale pink or hyacinth blue, is probably an ancient oriental garden variety and arrived in the West in 1789. It is also excellent in containers.

Pelargonium GERANIUM

'Geraniums', still so called as they were once placed in that closely related genus, have been grown since *Pelargonium triste* (the 'sad-coloured' pelargonium) arrived in Europe in 1631. Like most species, it comes from South Africa. Unusually, it is tuberous-rooted, with sprays of delicate yellow and brown flowers. It is not especially showy, but worth growing for its powerfully sweet scent of cloves and other spices, strongest at night.

By the early years of the nineteenth century, the pelargonium had become 'the chief of flowering plants suitable for the parterre'. Many nineteenth-century varieties still exist, including 'Happy Thought' (green-margined leaves with a gold heart, and brilliant scarlet flowers), 'Freak of Nature' (a dwarf variety), 'Crystal Palace Gem', 'Golden Harry

Hieover' (fine yellow leaves with a greyish horseshoe, often used for edgings in the parterre), 'Mrs Parker', 'Caroline Schmidt' (with almost silver leaves), 'Lass o' Gowrie', 'Miss Burdett Coutts', 'Mangle's Variegated' (probably the most famous of them all, a dwarf variety with dark green, silver-splashed leaves) and 'Mrs Pollock' (yellow foliage with a horseshoe of reddish bronze).

Ivy-leafed pelargoniums also began to arrive in the early 1700s, and some of the cultivars have been long-lasting; 'L'Elégante', silver-edged and variegated-leafed, with pale violet flowers, was praised in 1887 and is still around.

Regal pelargoniums, called 'Martha Washingtons' in the US, seem to have originated at Sandringham House (whence the 'regal' association) and reached less grand windowsills around 1877.

Scented-leafed pelargoniums began to arrive in Europe in the seventeenth century, but most appeared in the next. *Pelargonium* 'Fragrans', a hybrid with pine-scented grey-green leaves, has been known since 1645. The common rose-scented *P. graveolens* was introduced in 1774, as was the even rosier *P. radula*. Peppermint and lemon-scented types have been around since the late eighteenth century, the variegated 'Lady Plymouth' since 1802 and the deliciously orange-peel-scented 'Prince of Orange' since at least 1880.

Verbena VERBENA

The half-hardy perennial bedding verbena (*Verbena* × *hybrida*) makes marvellous potfuls under glass, many pleasantly perfumed and all colourful. They are the result of crosses between species introduced from South America between 1826 and 1837. Hybrids, popular by 1844, include the scented and soft pink 'Silver Anne', the deep purple 'Hidcote' and the loud scarlet 'Huntsman' – all modern names for plants available from the 1850s. Many look good combined with white Paris daisies and perhaps grey-foliaged helichrysums. Under glass, greenfly can be a nuisance.

Below left: *Hydrangea paniculata* and most other shrubby hydrangeas grow well – and look good – in large tubs or pots.

Below right: These striking verbenas – the purple 'Huntsman' and scarlet 'Hidcote' – make a startling combination in a medium to large pot.

A VICTORIAN CONSERVATORY

Though the house and garden, deep in the Cotswolds, are old, this conservatory is a mere stripling of 12 years. It replaces a handsome vine house of 1848 which had (as greenhouses and conservatories do) reached the end of its days. The new structure follows the plan of the earlier one, and even incorporates its fireplace (though the owner complains that this smokes if the wind is from the wrong direction). The conservatory is divided by a partition into two sections.

Below: The entrancing antique Wardian case – a conservatory within a conservatory.

Right: The wall fountain belonged to the original conservatory; the handsome weather-cock is part of the owner's collection. The pale-flowered orchid is *Dendrobium paxtonii*.

Above: The scented flowers of *Passiflora caerulea*, an easily grown antique climber.

Below: Many ferns make excellent conservatory plants for shady corners; they were Victorian favourites.

Above: A stone shepherd, one of the many decorative antiques that adorn this indoor garden, stands shaded by grapevines.

One, barely heated, is used for the owner's collection of prize-winning show auriculas – the conservatory doors are left open all summer to prevent overheating. The other section is heated and allows the luxuriant growth of exotic climbers and pot plants. It is filled with containers growing mostly antique plants, as well as some well-chosen antiques. It makes a perfect place to sit on a summer's morning – or a winter's evening, with the fire lit, and a few candles.

The conservatory's most important element is light. Being south-facing, it is potentially as hot as Death Valley in summer, but instead of blinds creating shade, here it is the plants themselves that perform the function, producing a result much more sympathetic to human inhabitants and to the plants growing beneath. However, plant maintenance is more work than looking after blinds.

In this conservatory, the climbers run over a free-standing metal arbour that has been specially designed for their support, but it is easy to make something that gives a similar effect. Simply provide the roof beams with wires along their length and support the wires from brackets so that they are at least 15cm (6in) from the glass; this allows the leaves plenty of room without

Above: The headily perfumed and easily grown double datura (*Brugmansia candida* 'Plena') will flower well into early winter.

Right: The division between the barely heated and the well-heated areas in this dual-purpose conservatory. As it would have done in Victorian times, the Wardian case provides an extra layer of insulation for the plants it contains.

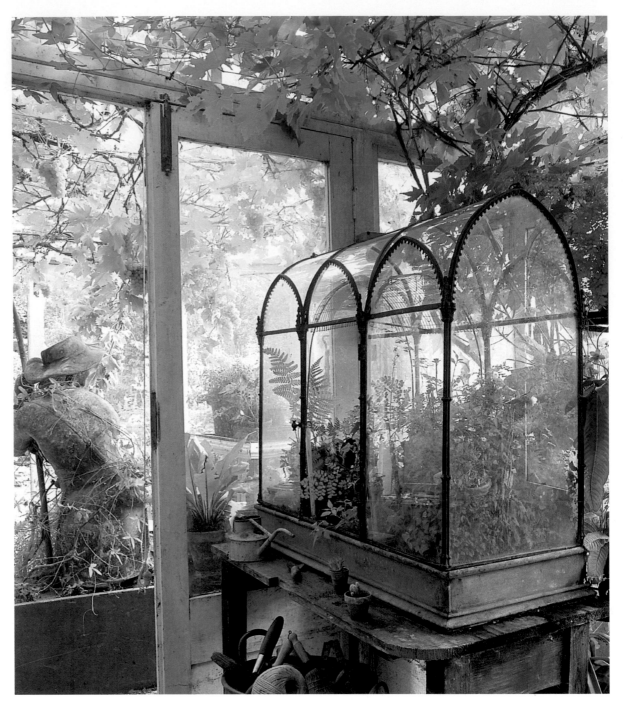

touching the glass itself. The climbers can then be trained up the wires, with much of their side growth kept pruned back.

Most of the climbers grown here are vines. One is eight years old; the other is a shoot that springs from the remaining roots of one planted by the original conservatory. Vines need a substantial amount of work through the season if they are to remain pest free, and to give a good crop. If you prefer less effort, use a pest-resistant plant, like a perfumed jasmine (*Jasminum sambac* or *J. officinale*). All are vigorous, and need thinning after each wave of flowers, but do not need spraying. Alternatively – and especially if you want to use the conservatory during the winter and need more light – grow vigorous climbers often treated as annuals: morning glories, or the marvellously perfumed moonflower (*Ipomoea alba*).

Another good climber in this conservatory is *Plumbago capensis*. Easy and fast-growing, it often puts on 1.5–2m (5ft–6ft 6in) growth in a season. The china blue (or, more rarely, white) flowers last several weeks, though bunches are produced through summer and autumn. They have, alas, no perfume. For that, try *Hoya carnosa*, which will hardly flower when it is growing fast in a large pot, but blooms when it is starved. The pinkish waxen flowers have an overwhelming smell in the evening. If that is too much, try the gentler but glorious scent of the passionflowers. The one here is the lovely antique *Passiflora caerulea*, which is almost hardy, with pale greeny-blue flowers.

Once green summer shade is provided for, add to the generosity of greenery by using shelving or tiered stands to pack in yet more foliage, especially of shade-tolerant plants. Though some of the shelving systems in this conservatory are of the late nineteenth century, modern examples can be just as effective and are more easily found. Fill them, as here, with lots of pots of streptocarpus. Easy from seed or cuttings, the plants thrive in these conditions and have long flowering seasons, dramatic flowers and large, splendidly veined leaves. They seem to enjoy close contact and do well crammed on to shelves and tables.

An amusing contrast here is provided by the little 'bead plant' (*Nertera granadensis*), with its tiny leaves and large red berries. Popular in Victorian garden rooms, it is easily grown from seed, or is sometimes found in garden centres. It does best if watered from below; the leaves and stems rot if watered from above.

The effect of any container garden, whether outdoors or under glass, is partly determined by the 'props': seating, statuary, types of container and so on. Here, decorative antiques (the owner deals in antiquities) combine delightfully with the plants. Choose things that won't be too damaged by high humidity or the occasional misdirection of a hosepipe or spray.

The most exciting piece is, of course, the Wardian case, providing a delightful conservatory within a conservatory. Wardian cases first appeared in the late 1820s, the invention of one Nathaniel Ward, and were used for growing plants that hated conditions in the average sitting room. They then became immensely important as a means of transporting jungle plants around the world, and were instrumental in the introduction of many plants to European and North American conservatories, especially ferns and orchids. This one is an heirloom, having once belonged to the owner's great-uncle, who used it to house part of a remarkable orchid collection.

Above: Cymbidiums like this were being hybridized from the 1850s; this one is called 'Rosanette'.

Left: Trails of *Plumbago capensis* almost smother the fireplace and make a luscious canopy for the owner's favourite chair.

FAGUS

Deciduous tree, can make hedges to 12m (40ft) high. Foliage can be variegated or purple. Sun or part shade; hardy. Propagate by seed, cuttings. Widely available.

FOENICULUM

Mostly herbaceous perennials, up to 2m (6ft) × 1m (3ft). Flowers in summer and autumn, leaves blue-green or purple. Sun or part shade; hardy. Good garden soil for bulb-forming varieties, ordinary for others, average to moist. Widely available.

FRITILLARIA

Bulbs, up to 1m (3ft) in *F. imperialis* and *F. persica*, usually half that. Flowers in spring, in white, yellow, orange, purple, sometimes chequered. Sun or partial shade; most antiques hardy. Propagate by seed or division. Widely available. *F. imperialis* 'Crown on Crown' from:
Rupert Bowlby, Gatton,
Reigate RH2 0TA

HEDERA HELIX

Self-clinging climber, evergreen, rarely a bush form. Both height and spread indeterminate. Flowers in winter; large range of leaf forms and variegations. Sun or deep shade; hardy. Do not grow up damp or poorly mortared walls. Propagate by cuttings. Widely available; unusual varieties from:
Fibrex Nurseries,
Honeybourne Road, Pebworth,
Stratford upon Avon CV37 8XT

HELIOTROPIUM

Weak shrubs, 60cm (2ft) × 1m (3ft). Flowers whenever in growth, in mauves, white. Sun, part shade; tender. Rich soil, average to moist. Cut back when it becomes too leggy. Propagate by cuttings, seed. Widely available; 'Gatton Park' from:
Merriments Gardens, Hawkhurst
Road, Hurst Green TN19 7RA

HELLEBORUS

Herbaceous perennials to low sub-shrubs, up to 60cm (2ft) × indefinite. Flowers borne winter/spring, in white, green, shades of pink. *H. niger* needs good soil and light; *H. foetidus* prefers shade; all hardy. Propagate *H. niger* by division, others by seed. These and *H. orientalis* widely available.

HEMEROCALLIS

Herbaceous perennial, up to 1.25m (4ft) × indeterminate. Flowers in summer, in yellow to rust red. Part shade; hardy. Divide clumps every few seasons. Propagate by division for named sorts; otherwise seed. Widely available; variegated 'Kwanso' from:
Monksilver Nursery, Oakington Road,
Cottenham BD4 4TW

HESPERIS

Biennial, up to 1.5m (4ft 6in) × 75cm (2ft 6in). Flowers summer, pure white to pale purple. Sun or part shade; hardy. Propagate by seed (self-sows well). Widely available.

HYDRANGEA

Deciduous shrubs. Size varies with species, but hortensias to 1.5m (4ft 6in). Flowers in late summer/autumn, in reds, blues, mauves, white. Part or full shade; hardy. Remove old flowerheads without damaging buds below. Propagate by cuttings. Widely available; 'Sir Joseph Banks' from:
Hickling Heath Nursery,
Sutton Road, Hickling NR12 0AS

ILEX

Evergreen trees, to 10m (33ft) × 5m (16ft), though commonly pruned. Grown for autumn berries and foliage, variously shaped and variegated. Sun or shade; hardy except in extreme winters. Propagate by seed or summer cuttings. Many varieties from:
Highfield Hollies, Highfield Farm,
Hatch Lane, Liss GU33 7NH

IPOMOEA

Annual, sometimes perennial, twining climber. Indeterminate size, but at least 3m (10ft). Flowers begin when stems are 1m (3ft) high, in blues, magenta, purples, white. Sun; tender. Rich soil, average to moist; plenty of space. Propagate by seed. Widely available.

IRIS

Semi-evergreen rhizomatous perennial, or bulbs, up to 1.5m (5ft) × indefinite. Flowers in early spring to high summer, in shades of blue, yellow or white. Sun; *I. germanica* forms, *I. foetidissima* and a number of bulbous varieties hardy. Free-draining sandy soil, dry to average moisture. Rhizomatous sorts need dividing every few seasons. Propagate by division, seed. All widely available.

JASMINUM

Twining shrubs, often evergreen, sometimes scramblers. Indeterminate size. *J. nudiflorum* flowers in winter, others in spring under glass, high summer outdoors; flowers are white, yellow, rarely pink. Sun or part shade; some species tender, others hardy. Rich garden soil, allow plenty of space. Propagate by cuttings. Most varieties widely available; *J. sambac* from:
Reads Nursery, Hales Hall,
Loddon NR14 6QW

LATHYRUS ODORATA

Climbing annual, up to 3m (10ft). Flowers borne in mid to late summer, in purples, blues, pinks, usually mixed. Sun; dies after flowering, though young plants can be overwintered outdoors. Rich garden soil, average to moist. Deadhead regularly if you want a long flowering season. Propagate by seed. Many varieties widely available; 'Painted Lady' from:
Glebe Cottage Plants, Pixie Lane,
Warkleigh, Umberleigh EX37 9DH

LAURUS

Suckering evergreen tree, usually pruned, often as topiary. Height to 10m (33ft), width to 7m (23ft). Flowers small, yellowish, in spring; foliage usually green, narrow in 'Angustifolia', yellow in 'Aurea'. Sun; killed by severe frost. Propagate by cuttings, seed. Widely available.

LAVANDULA

Short-lived evergreen bush. Dwarf sorts to 20cm (8in), large ones to 1m (3ft) in both height and spread. Flowers in summer, in mauves, white, pale pink. Sun; hardy. Propagate by cuttings in spring, or by seed. Many varieties widely available.

LILIUM

Bulbous perennials, up to 2m (6ft 6in) high. Flowers in early to high summer, in white, purple, red, yellow; often spotted. Sun or part shade; all species listed are hardy. Average to peaty soil, average moisture. Watch for tobacco mosaic virus. Propagate by seed, or bulb scales treated as cuttings. Most varieties widely available. *L bulbiferum* may be grown from seed; alternatively bulbs are available from:
Van Tubergen Ltd, Bressingham,
Diss IP22 2AB

LONICERA

Twining shrubs, some evergreen. Indeterminate size. Flowers late spring to early summer, with outer surfaces of petals in cream, yellow, red or purple. Best in sun; hardy. Watch for aphids. Propagate by layering. Widely available.

LUNARIA

Biennial, or perennial in *L. rediviva*, 1m (3ft) × 60cm (2ft). Flowers lilac, purple or white in late spring/early summer. In *L. annua* leaves may be variegated. Sun or shade; hardy. Often self-sows. Widely available.

LUPINUS

Annuals, herbaceous perennials, rarely sub-shrubs, up to 1.5m (5ft) × indeterminate. Flowers in summer, in blues, mauves, yellows, white. Sun or part shade; hardy. Tree lupin short-lived, so save a few seeds. Propagate by seed, or division in perennials. Widely available. Tree lupin varieties from:
Madrona Nursery,
Bethersden TN26 3DD

LYCOPERSICON

Herbaceous, often treated as annual, weak shrubs to 2m (6ft 6in), or rampant climbers. Flowers within a few months of sowing, fruits variously shaped, in reds, yellows or white. Sun or partial shade; tender. Rich garden soil, average to moist, under glass. Tap open flowers to ensure pollination. Old 'Marmande' types widely available.

MALUS

Deciduous tree, size varies with variety and the stock used for grafting, but can be up to 10m (33ft) high and across. Mostly pruned to size. Flowers spring, fruit ripening in autumn to late winter, in greens, yellows, reds, russets. Sun; hardy. Specialized forms need careful pruning in winter and summer. Propagate by grafting. Old sorts from:
Keepers Nursery, Gallants Lane,
East Farleigh, Maidstone ME15 0LE; or
Scotts Nurseries, Merriott TA16 5PL

MENTHA

Mostly rampant herbaceous perennials, up to 1m (3ft) high × indefinite. Flowers late summer, leaves variously frilled, variegated. Sun or shade; hardy. Invasive, so best grown in isolation or with other vigorous herbs. Propagate by division or seed. Widely available.

MESPILUS

Small deciduous tree, 5m (16ft) × 4m (13ft). Flowers in spring, fruit ripens late autumn; flowers cream, fruit warm brown, leaves bronze. Sun or part shade; not reliably hardy in bitter winters. Propagate by grafting or seed. Many varieties from:
J. Tweedie Fruit Trees,
Maryfield Road Nursery, Maryfield,
near Terregles DG2 9YH

NARCISSUS

Clump-forming bulbs, up to 40cm (1ft 4in) × indeterminate. Flowers late winter into early summer, in yellows, sometimes cream, rarely white. Sun or partial shade; all except 'Paper Whites' hardy. Average to well-drained soil, average moisture. Clumps eventually stop flowering – divide every few seasons. Propagate by division. 'Queen Anne's Double' from:
Copford Bulbs, Dorsetts, Birch Road,
Copford, Colchester CO6 1DR

NICOTIANA

Often perennial in warmth, generally treated as annuals, up to 2m (6ft 6in) × 1m (3ft). Flowers summer and into autumn (winter under glass), in white, pinks, mauves, green. Sun; tender. Rich garden soil, average to moist. Blackfly can be a nuisance. Propagate by seed. Widely available.

OCIMUM

Mostly annuals, some perennials. Height and spread 30cm (1ft). Flowers late summer, leaves greens or purple, flat, wrinkled. Sun; tender. Best in rich garden soil , average to moist. Grow fast to avoid plants running to flower. Will not grow outdoors in northern parts of Britain. Widely available.

OENOTHERA

Biennial or perennial. *O. biennis* to 1m (3ft) × 45cm (1ft 6in); *O. acaulis* 30cm (1ft) × 30cm (1ft). Flowers early to late summer, in yellows, sometimes white or apricot. Sun or part shade; hardy. Widely available.

OMPHALODES

Creeping herbaceous perennial (*O. cappadocicum* evergreen). Height to 20cm (8in), spread indefinite. Flowers in spring, in blue, rarely white. Part to full shade; hardy. Propagate by division. Widely available.

ORIGANUM

Mostly herbaceous perennials, 45cm (1ft 6in) × 1m (3ft). Flowers summer, leaves in greens, yellows, variegated. Sun or part shade; hardy. Propagate by division or seed. Widely available.

PAEONIA

Herbaceous perennials or shrubs. Herbaceous sorts to 75cm (2ft 6in) × 1m (3ft); shrubs to height and spread of 2m (6ft 6in). Flowers in early to high summer, in white, yellows, pinks and reds. Part shade; hardy. Propagate named herbaceous sorts by division, rarely seed; shrubs by seed or grafting. Good range from:
Kelways Ltd, Langport TA10 9EZ

PAPAVER

Annuals, biennials or herbaceous perennials, sometimes free-spreading, up to 1m (3ft) × (in *P. orientale*) indeterminate. Flowers in early summer, in white, scarlets, pinks, purples. Sun; perennial sorts hardy. Rich garden soil. Divide *P. orientale* every few seasons. Propagate herbaceous sorts by root cuttings, others by seed. Widely available; old double from:
Four Seasons, Forncett St Mary,
Norwich NR16 1JT

PELARGONIUM

Mostly low shrubs, usually evergreen (deciduous in bad conditions). Size varies with variety, but up to 2m (6ft 6in), more with support. Flowers in all growing seasons, in white, pink, reds, mauves; foliage very variable. Sun, part shade; mostly tender. Needs frequent pruning to keep in shape. Propagate by cuttings or seed. Good range from:
Fibrex Nurseries Ltd,
Honeybourne Road, Pebwirth,
Stratford upon Avon CV37 8XT

PETROSELINUM

Herbaceous biennial, before flowering 30cm (1ft) × same. Flowers in second spring, leaves flat or frilled. Sun, part shade; hardy except in severe winters. In cold gardens, ensure their survival by overwintering a few plants under a cloche. Widely available.

PHASEOLUS

Climbing or bushy annual (perennial in warm climates), up to 5m (16ft) × indeterminate. Flowers summer, autumn; will crop to first frosts, in white, pink, tomato red, pods in greens, yellows, purples, or variously streaked and splashed in these colours. Best in sheltered, sunny places; not hardy. Prefers rich soil, average to wet. Sow seed outdoors a few weeks after last frost. Widely available.

PHILADELPHUS

Deciduous bushes, to 5m (16ft) × 3m (10ft). Flowers in early summer, in white. Sun, partial shade; hardy. Prune after flowering. Propagate by cuttings. Widely available.

PISUM

Annual, bushy or climbing. Size varies with variety, climbers to 3m (10ft). Pods mostly greens, sometimes purple. Sun or partial shade; most sorts not hardy. Rich garden soil. Pick over crop every few days to keep plants producing. Widely available.

PRIMULA

Herbaceous perennials, auriculas evergreen, those listed up to 30cm (1ft) × indeterminate. Flowers late winter to early summer, white, yellows, reds, rarely green. Part shade or full shade; hardy. Border soil or leafmould, average moisture for auriculas, average to moist for others. Primroses need dividing each season after flowering. Propagate all varieties either by seed (sow in autumn outdoors in pots) or division. Many forms widely available. *Primula* 'Marie Crousse' and many others from:
Potterton and Martin, The Cottage
Nursery, Moortown Road, Nettleton,
Caistor LN7 6HX
Many old auriculas from:
Field House Nurseries, Leake Road,
Gotham NG11 OJN or
Brenda Hyatt, 1 Toddington Crescent,
Bluebell Hill, Chatham ME5 9QT

PRUNUS AVIUM

Eventually becomes a large deciduous tree, reaching a height of up to 14m (45ft). Flowers spring, fruiting in early to high summer. Flowers white, autumn foliage golden or scarlet. Sun or partial shade (though morellos will fruit in full shade); hardy. Can be pruned as fans. Propagate by grafting. Many forms available from:
Keepers Nursery, Gallants Court,
Gallants Lane, East Farleigh,
Maidstone ME15 OLE

PRUNUS DOMESTICA

Deciduous trees, can reach 10m (33ft), but often pruned smaller. Flowers spring, sometimes early; fruits summer; in autumn foliage sometimes bronze or yellow. Sun; hardy. In cool gardens, choice sorts, especially gages, best trained against a wall. Propagate by grafting, or by seed for myrobalans and some plums and gages.
J. Tweedie Fruit Trees, Maryfield Road,
Maryfield, near Terregles DG2 9TH

PRUNUS PERSICA

Small tree, can be grown potted, up to 5m (16ft) × 3m (10ft). Flowers early spring (watch for frost damage), fruits midsummer to early autumn, in pink, creams, reds, yellows. Shelter, full sun, good against a sunny wall; fully hardy. Often flowers before bees emerge, so hand pollinate. Propagate by grafting, though 'Pèche de vigne' and nectarines come true from seed.
Ken Muir, Honeypot Farm, Rectory
Road, Weeley Heath CO16 9BJ

PYRUS

Often large, long-lived, deciduous trees, up to 12m (40ft) × 7m (23ft). Flowers spring, fruit ripening summer to late winter, autumn foliage sometimes butter yellow. Sun; hardy. Easily pruned to size, or to make espaliers or fans. Propagate by grafting.
Scotts Nurseries (Merriott) Ltd,
Merriott TA16 5PL

RANUNCULUS

Corms or herbaceous perennials, up to 1m (3ft) × indefinite. Flowers in early summer, in white, scarlet, yellow. Sun or part shade; cormous sorts lifted in summer, others hardy. Perennials need dividing every few seasons. Propagate by seed or division. Corms of many varieties widely available; *R. aconitifolius* 'Flore Pleno' from:
Green Farm Plants, Bentley,
Farnham GU10 5JX

RIBES X UVA-CRISPA VAR. RECLINATUM

Deciduous, spiny bushes. Height and spread to 2m (6ft 6in). Flowers spring, fruiting early to midsummer; fruits in black, greens, yellows; smooth or prickly. Sun or partial shade; hardy. Can be pruned as standards. Watch for sawfly. Propagate by cuttings, seed.
R. V. Roger Ltd, The Nurseries,
Pickering YO18 7HG

ROSA

Climbing roses: deciduous or semi-evergreen, usually thorny scramblers. Size varies with variety but can get to 10m (33ft) or more. Flowers in early summer, sometimes late summer, in white, yellows, pinks. Sun, though some will also flower well in shade; fully hardy, though there will be occasional losses below –10°C (14°F). For antique varieties, pruning is not vital; instead, thin out the whole plant. Propagate by cuttings.

Shrub roses: shrubs, sometimes lax. Size varies with variety, but up to 2.5m (8ft) × 2m (6ft 6in). Flowers in late mid to high summer for most single-season varieties, in white, rose pinks, purples. Best in full sun, although will tolerate partial shade; fully hardy, though occasional losses below – 10°C (14°F). Rich soil best, average moisture.

Pruning is important – shrub and species roses should be pruned lightly, since they flower on wood two years old or more. Prune every year by cutting out some of the oldest stems right down to the base, allowing space for strong new shoots to grow. With varieties that flower only once, prune after flowering; with those that repeat flower, do it in autumn. Over a four-year period, the whole bush should have been recycled.

Alternatively leave the bush as a tangle, eventually using a hedge-trimmer to cut the whole thing down to about 15cm (6in) and then letting it regrow. Propagate by cuttings in late summer or early autumn, though use seed for new varieties.

Many old gardens have ancient roses in them, which may come easily from cuttings. Don't ignore them because they are now anonymous. In addition to those included in the roses chapter of this book, other good varieties worth seeking out are: 'Ville de Bruxelles', 'Madame Legras de St Germain', 'Tuscany Superb', 'Robert le Diable', 'Pompon Blanc Parfait'.

Sources:
David Austin Roses, Bowling Green Lane, Albrighton, Wolverhampton WV7 3HB;
Peter Beales Roses, London Road, Attleborough NR17 1AY;
Just Roses, Beales Lane, Northiam TN31 6QY

ROSMARINUS

Evergreen bush. Upright sorts to height and spread of 1.5m (4ft 6in). Flowers in early summer in purples, white, pale pink. Sun or part shade; hardy in mild winters. Propagate by cuttings, seed. Widely available.

SANGUINARIA

Creeping herbaceous perennial, 20cm (8in) × indefinite. Flowers early spring, white. Part to full shade; hardy. Any good garden soil, average moisture. Propagate by division. Widely available.

SANTOLINA

Low evergreen bushes. Height and spread 1m (3ft). Flowers in summer, in cream or yellow, usually removed. Requires sun; hardy. Average to poor soil, average to dry. Propagate by cuttings. Widely available.

SCILLA

Bulb, up to 40cm (1ft 4in). Flowers spring, in blue, rarely shades of purple, white. Sun; all listed varieties hardy. Propagate by division or seed. Widely available; *S. peruviana* from:
Monocot Nursery, Jacklands, Jacklands Bridge, Tickenham, Clevedon BS21 6SG

SILENE

Clump-forming herbaceous perennials, up to 45cm (18in) × indeterminate. Flowers in late spring/early summer, in white, rose pinks. Part shade; fully hardy. Watch for blackfly on flowering stems. Propagate double sorts by division, single ones by seed. Try also the double form *S. maritima*. It and other listed varieties widely available.

SKIMMIA

Evergreen bushes, 1m (3ft) × 1.5m (4ft 6in). Flowers spring, though often grown for autumn berries, in red, pinkish or white. Partial or full shade; hardy. Male and female plants needed for berries. Propagate by seed or summer cuttings. Widely available.

SPINACIA

Leafy annual. Size varies with variety, but height and spread to 40cm (1ft 4in). Leaves smooth, sometimes 'savoyed'. Sun or shade; tender. Rich, moist garden soil – do not let it dry out. Sow small amounts through growing period. Widely available.

TAXUS

The best choice of hedging plant for large hedges; otherwise, left unpruned, it makes a small tree 10–15m (33–50ft) × 5–10m (16–33ft). Flowers insignificant, foliage dark green to brownish yellow. Tolerates full shade; fully hardy. Propagate either by cuttings or by seed. Widely available.

THYMUS

Creeping perennials, or small shrublets. Size varies with species, but height and spread to 30cm (1ft). Flowers summer, mauve or white, leaves various greens, yellows, variegated. Sun; most species hardy. Average to poor soil, average to dry. Propagate by cuttings or from seed. Most listed varieties – and others – widely available.

TROPAEOLUM

Climbers, often treated as annuals in cold countries, to around 3m (10ft). Flowers summer, early autumn, in oranges, scarlet, reds, yellow. Sun or part shade; many tender, though *T. speciosum* and some other tuberous sorts hardy. Propagate by seed. *T. maius, T. peregrinum, T. speciosum* widely available; *T.* 'Hermine Grasshoff' available from:
Cottage Nurseries, Thoresthorpe, Alfrod LN13 0HX

TULIPA

Bulbs, up to 60cm (2ft). Flowers winter if forced, spring to early summer outdoors, in every colour except blue. Sun, except *T. sylvestris*, for which part shade; most are frost-hardy in dryish soils, but are commonly lifted in summer. *T. acuminata* and *T. clusiana* best lifted and dried in winter. Propagate by division; florists' sorts were grown from seed. Widely available; florists' sorts circulate between growers. *T. acuminata* from:
Rupert Bowlby, Gatton, Reigate RH2 0TA

VERATRUM

Herbaceous perennials, up to 2m (6ft 6in) × 1m (3ft). Flowers in summer, in green, white, blackish. Part to full shade; hardy. Rich soil gives best foliage, average to moist soil. Slugs can ruin foliage. Propagate by seed (sow outdoors in autumn) or division. *V. album* and *V. nigrum* are both widely available.

VERBENA

Sprawling evergreen sub-shrub. Size varies with variety, often to 45cm (1ft 6in) × indeterminate. Flowers summer, autumn, in mauves, reds, white, often with coloured eye. Sun or part shade; tender. Feed well, prune when untidy. Propagate by cuttings or seed.
Steventon Road Nurseries, Steventon Road, East Hanney, Wantage OX12 0HS

VIBURNUM

Deciduous or evergreen shrubs. *V. opulus* to 7m (22ft) × 3m (10ft); *V. tinus* to 5m (16ft) × 3m (10ft). *V. opulus* flowers in summer; *V. tinus* autumn to spring, in white, but both grown for scarlet berries. Partial to full shade; hardy. Any soil, average moisture. Put several plants together to ensure good crops of berries. Propagate by seed or cuttings. Widely available.

VINCA

Low, sprawling evergreens, up to 30cm (1ft) × indefinite. Flowers in late spring, leaves may be variously variegated, flowers in blues, purples. Sun or shade; hardy. Watch that they do not shade out nearby plants. Propagate by division or cuttings. Widely available.

VIOLA

Mat-forming perennials, 30cm (1ft) × indeterminate. Flowers in late spring to autumn, depending on species and variety, in white, yellow, blues, purples, reds. *V. odorota* best in shade, others in sun or partial shade; fully hardy. Good rich moist soil. Spray regularly for viola midge and greenfly. Propagate by division, cuttings or seed. Violas generally widely available; *V. odorata* varieties from:
Paradise Centre, Twinstead Road, Lamarsh, Bures CO8 5EX

VITIS

Rampant deciduous climber. Virtually indefinite height and spread, usually hard pruned. Lightly fragrant flowers in spring, fruit ripening in summer or autumn; autumn foliage sometimes bronzes; fruits green, gold, purples. Sun; hardy. Vegetation needs constant thinning during summer; bunches of fruit need thinning as each berry grows. Propagate by cuttings.
Reads Nursery, Hales Hall, Loddon NR14 6QW

OTHER GENERAL BULB SUPPLIERS

For specifically antique varieties of bulbs, consult lists like that of *Thomas Etty Esq.*, who specializes in antique bulbs as well as the seed of antique vegetable varieties.
Thomas Etty Esq.,
Seedman and Bulb Merchant,
45 Forde Avenue, Bromley BR1 3EY

Avon Bulbs,
Burnt House Farm, Mid-Lambrook,
South Petherton TA13 5HE

Broadleigh Garden, Bishops Hull,
Taunton TA4 1AE

VEGETABLES

A list of ancient, non-commercialized vegetables is available from:
The Henry Doubleday Research Association, Ryton Gardens, Ryton-on-Dunsmore, Coventry CV8 3LG
Tel: 0203 303517

HERBACEOUS PLANTS

Bressingham Plant Centres, Bressingham, Diss IP22 2AB

Holden Clough Nursery, Holden, Bolton-by-Bowland, Clitheroe BB7 4PF

Hopleys Plants Ltd, High Street, Much Hadham SG10 6BU

GROWING FROM SEED

Many antique garden plants, shrubs and trees, as well as border flowers and wild garden plants, are easily grown from seed. For vegetable and salad plants, it is, of course, the only way. Raising any plant from seed really needs only a little skill, and can easily furnish large numbers if you want to cover the ground quickly. The following suppliers have especially good lists:

Chiltern Seeds, Bortree Stile, Ulverston LA12 7PB

Thompson and Morgan, Poplar Lane, Ipswich IP8 3BU

B & T World Seeds, Whitnell House, Fiddington, Bridgewater TA5 1JE

Suffolk Herbs, Monks Farm, Pantlings Road, Coggeshall Road, Kelvedon CO5 9PG

USEFUL ORGANIZATIONS AND SOCIETIES

The Royal Horticultural Society, PO Box 313, 80 Vincent Square, London SW1P 2PE

The Royal National Rose Society, The Gardens of the Rose, Chiswell Green, St Albans AL2 3NR

The Cottage Garden Society, 5 Nixon Close, Thornhill, Dewsbury WF12 0JA
Subscription £5 per person. Seed scheme; a good journal; regional group.

Friends of Brogdale,
The Brogdale Horticultural Trust, Brogdale Farm, Faversham ME13 8XZ
Tel 01795 535286 Fax 01795 531710
Brogdale Farm holds the major UK collection of fruit species, holds regular tasting days and will supply propagation material. The collection holds large numbers of 'antiques'.

The Garden History Society, 5 The Knoll, Hereford HR1 1RU
Tel: 01432 354479
Though rather academic in its approach, the excellent magazine often has much to interest 'antique plant' gardeners.

National Auricula and Primula Society, 67 Warnham Court Road, Carshalton Beeches SM5 3ND
If you can't have enough of auriculas and antique 'lookalike' primulas, this is worth joining.

National Council for the Conservation of Plants and Gardens, The Pines, Wisley Garden, Woking GU23 6QB.
An organization devoted to collecting, and ensuring the survival of, old garden plants. Many of the 'National Collections' are easily visited (see below) and can help you identify any plant you suspect of being an antique.

NATIONAL COLLECTIONS

The formation of these specialist collections – usually of particular genera, more rarely of whole groups, and concentrating most frequently on fruit trees, is most developed in the UK, but is also starting throughout Western Europe and in North America. Full lists of UK collections can be found in The Plant Finder, and often in the booklets issued by the English and Scottish 'Gardens Schemes'.

Some important genera included in this book can be seen (usually by prior arrangement) at the following locations:

Acer (170 Japanese cultivars)
Westonbirt Arboretum, Tetbury GL8 8QS Tel 01666 880 220

Agapanthus (90)
R. Fulcher, Bicton College of Agriculture, East Budleigh EX9 7BY
Tel 01395 568353

Anemone
(30 hupehensis and japonica hybrids)
D. G. Barker, 'Stone Pine', Hyde Lane, Danbury, Chelmsford CM3 4JL
Tel 01245 223232

Aquilegia (65 species & 55 cultivars)
J. Drake, Hardwicke House, Fen Ditton, Cambridge CB5 8TF
Tel 01223 292246

Buxus (86 species and cultivars)
R. Kew Collection, at Greenholm Nurseries Ltd, Lampley Road, Kingston Seymour, Clevedon BS21 6XS
Tel 01934 833350

Clematis (170 species and cultivars)
Treasures of Tenbury Ltd, Burford House, Tenbury Wells WR15 8HQ
Tel 01584 810777

Crocus (120 species and cultivars)
D. Stephens, 'Sherwood', Bruce Common Road, Leigh RH2 8NS
Tel 01306 611420

Dianthus
(140 and more old fashioned pinks):
Mrs S. Hughes, Kingstone Cottage, Weston under Penyard, Ross on Wye HR9 7NX Tel 01989 565267

Erythronium
(25 species & 18 cultivars)
Mr J. Phillips, 10 Highwood, Driffield YO25 7YX Tel 01377 241082

Hepatica (9 species and 70 cultivars)
M. D. Myers, Fairview, Smelthouses, Summerbridge, near Harrogate HG3 4DH Tel 01423 780291

Lavandula (52 species and cultivars)
Chris Yates, The Scented Garden, Gardens Cottage, Littlebredy, Dorchester DT2 9HG
Tel 01308 482307

Lychnis (8 species and 7 cultivars)
Jean Sambrook, Garden Cottage, 214 Ruxley Lane, West Ewell, Surrey Tel 0181 391 5144

Paeonia (65 pre-1900 cultivars)
Margaret Baber, Green Cottage, Redhill Lane, Lydney GL15 6BS
Tel 01594 841918

Papaver orientale (65 cultivars)
G. M. Hitchon, The Scottish Agricultural College, Auchincruive, Ayr KA6 5HN
Tel 01292 520331 ext. 432

Pelargonium (1677 cultivars)
Fibrex Nurseries, Honeybourne Road, Pebworth, Stratford-upon-Avon CV37 8XT Tel 01789 720788

Primula auricula
(125 border cultivars) *G. Nicolle, Rising Sun Cottage, Nolton Haven, Haverfordwest SA62 3NN*
Tel 01437 710542

Rosa (80 nineteenth-century cultivars of shrub roses)
National Trust for Scotland, Malleny House Garden, Balerno, Midlothian EH14 7AF Tel 0131 449 2283

Rosa (237 cultivars displaying the history of the European garden rose)
Professor J. G. Hawkes, University of Birmingham Botanic Gardens, Winterbourne, 56 Edgbaston Park Road, Edgbaston, Birmingham B15 2RT Tel 0121 414 5590

Rosmarinus (25 cultivars)
Pandora Thoresby, Yorkstock, Clifford Moor Road, Clifford, Wetherby LS236LD
Tel 01937 541387

Thymus (130 cultivars)
K. A. White, Hexham Herbs, Chesters Walled Garden, Chollerford, Hexham NE46 4BQ Tel 01434 681483

Tulipa (25 antique cultivars)
David Bromley, Moortown, near Wellington TF6 6JE
Tel 01952 770 205

Viola (66 viola and violetta cultivars)
K. Roberts, Roundhay Park, Canal Gardens, Princes Avenue, Leeds Tel 0113 26618504

Index

Author's Acknowledgments

I should like to thank a number of people who have been helpful in the writing of this book. One to whom I am especially grateful is Rand Lee, horticultural writer and editor, from Santa Fe, New Mexico. He is founder and current president of the American Dianthus Society and, with Nancy and Ira McDonald, co-creator of *The American Cottage Gardener*, a literary gardening quarterly devoted to interpreting the cottage-gardening style for North American climates and cultivars. He helped with many 'antique' queries. In the UK, I thank Ray Warner for his lists of antique bulb varieties and of vegetables that remain easily available to the gardener (which he has made more available still). I would also like to thank Carla Oldenburger-Ebbers, librarian at the University of Wageningen, Netherlands, for drawing my attention to some early sources of work about topiary.

Thanks go also to the owners of the gardens featured in book, particularly to David Beeson, for much information about meadows and meadow plants; to Roger Warner for help about the history and planting of his conservatory; to Dr Leslie and Mrs Cox for telling me about their decorative kitchen gardens (and for a plant of the red-leafed sorrel), as well as to Mr Jeffrey, gardener at the 'topiary garden'.

Picture Acknowledgments

1 Andrew Lawson; **2–3** Saxon Holt; **5** Bridgeman Art Library/Victoria & Albert Museum, London; **6** Bridgeman Art Library/Central Saint Martins College of Art & Design, London; **7** Bridgeman Art Library/Lindley Library, RHS, London; **8** Bridgeman Art Library/Lindley Library, RHS, London; **9** Bridgeman Art Library/Private Collection; **10** Bridgeman Art Library/Private Collection; **11** Bridgeman Art Library/Private Collection; **12** Bridgeman Art Library/Lindley Library, RHS, London; **13** Bridgeman Art Library/Linnean Society, London; **14** Bridgeman Art Library/Jessica Tcherepnine (living artist), Private Collection; **16** Bridgeman Art Library/Victoria & Albert Museum, London; **17** left Bridgeman Art Library/Private Collection; **17** right Bridgeman Art Library/Private Collection; **18** S & O Mathews (12 Rozelle Close, Littleton, Hampshire); **19** Bridgeman Art Library/Natural History Museum, London; **20** Bridgeman Art Library/Mallett Gallery; **21** Bridgeman Art Library/Lindley Library, RHS, London; **22** Andrew Lawson; **23** above S & O Mathews; **23** below Sunniva Harte; 24 Andrew Lawson; **25** above left John Glover; **25** above right S & O Mathews; **26** S & O Mathews; **27** Clive Nichols; **28** left S & O Mathews; **28** right Saxon Holt; **29** left S & O Mathews; **29** right John Glover; **30** above Jerry Harpur; **30–1** S & O Mathews; **30** below Harry Smith Collection; **31** John Glover; **32** Andrew Lawson; **33** above Sunniva Harte; **33** below Andrew Lawson; **34–5** Roger Foley (Colonial Williamsburg); **34** left John Glover; **35** right Andrew Lawson; **36** Sue Snell (Courtesy of The Charleston Trust, Sussex); **37** Andrew Lawson; **38** S & O Mathews; **39** Howard Rice; **40** left Andrew Lawson; **40** right S & O Mathews; **41** John Glover; **42** Photos Horticultural; **43** left John Glover; **43** right S & O Mathews (Little Court, Hampshire); **44** above Howard Rice; **44** below Ken Druse; **45** Jerry Harpur; **46** above S & O Mathews; **46** below Richard Felber (Pam Kay); **47** above left Richard Felber (Pam Kay); **47** above right Marianne Majerus; **47** below S & O Mathews; **48** above S & O Mathews; **48** left & right Richard Felber (Pam Kay); **49** Richard Felber (Pam Kay); **50** S & O Mathews (Stitches Farm House, Sussex); **51** Bridgeman Art Library/Private Collection; **52** Bridgeman Art Library/Christopher Wood Gallery, London; **56** Andrew Lawson; **57** left Andrew Lawson; **57** right Clive Nichols; **58** above Andrew Lawson; **58** below John Glover; **58–9** S & O Mathews; **60–1** Photos Horticultural; **60** left Clive Nichols; **61** Andrew Lawson; **62** left Andrew Lawson; **63** S & O Mathews; **64** Andrew Lawson; **65** Clive Nichols; **66–7** John Glover; **68** left John Glover; **68** right Andrew Lawson; **69** above S & O Mathews; **69** below Andrew Lawson; **70–1** Andrew Lawson; **70** above left Garden Matters; **70** below left Andrew Lawson; **71** Andrew Lawson; **74** above S & O Mathews; **76** Andrew Lawson (Levens Hall); **78** Bridgeman Art Library/John Spink Fine Watercolours, London; **80** John Glover (Toad Hall, Berkshire); **81** S & O Mathews; **82** above Jerry Harpur (La Casella, Alpes-Maritimes, France); **82** below John Glover (Hever Castle, Kent); **83** Andrew Lawson (Buckland Abbey, Devon, courtesy of The National Trust); **84** Jerry Harpur (La Casella, Alpes-Maritimes, France); **85** above right John Glover (Queen's Garden, Kew Gardens, Surrey); **85** centre right John Glover (RHS Wisley, Surrey); **85** below Jerry Harpur (Chevening, Kent); **86–9** Fritz von der Schulenburg/The Interior Archive (John Stefanidis); **90** The Garden Picture Library/Mayer/Le Scanff; **91** Bridgeman Art Library/Private Collection; **92** Bridgeman Art Library/Chris Beetles Ltd, London; **93** E.T. Archive; **94** Andrew Lawson; **96–7** The Garden Picture Library/Marijke Heuff; **96** left Harry Smith Collection; **97** right Andrew Lawson; **98–9** The Garden Picture Library/John Glover; **98** above left Saxon Holt; **98** below left Harry Smith Collection; **99** above right Andrew Lawson; **99** below right The Garden Picture Library/Sunniva Harte; **100** David Cavagnaro; **101** below left Photos Horticultural; **101** above left Jacqui Hurst; **101** right Andrew Lawson; **102** Andrew Lawson; **103** Andrew Lawson; **104** left The Garden Picture Library/David Russell; **104** right Andrew Lawson; **105** Andrew Lawson; **106–9** Sunniva Harte (Charleston Manor, Sussex); **110** Richard Felber (Robert Jakob & David White); **111** Bridgeman Art Library/Private Collection; **112** Sotheby's, London; **113** Bridgeman Art Library/Lindley Library, RHS, London; **115** above right The Garden Picture Library/Howard Rice; **115** below right Andrew Lawson; **116** left The Garden Picture Library/John Glover; **116** centre Photos Horticultural; **116** right John Glover; **117** left Jerry Harpur (Drummond Castle); **117** centre Photos Horticultural; **117** right The Garden Picture Library/Neil Holmes; **118** Sue Snell (Courtesy of The Charleston Trust, Sussex); **119** above Ken Druse; **119** below S & O Mathews; **120** above left Christian Sarramon; **120** below left Christian Sarramon; **120** right John Glover; **121** The Garden Picture Library/Lamontagne; **122–3** Saxon Holt; **122** left Juliette Wade; **122** right Sunniva Harte; **123** right Photos Horticultural; **124** Marijke Heuff (Huis Bingerden, Holland); **125** Clive Nichols (Cerney House Garden, Gloucestershire); **126** Andrew Lawson; **127** above Roger Foley (Colonial Williamsburg); **127** below centre Photos Horticultural; **127** below right John Glover; **127** right S & O Mathews; **127** below left S & O Mathews; **129** right John Glover; **131** above Roger Foley (Stratford Hall); **132** above S & O Mathews; **133** right The Garden Picture Library/Vaughan Fleming; **134** The Garden Picture Library/Linda Burgess; **135** Bridgeman Art Library/Fitzwilliam Museum, University of Cambridge; **136** Bridgeman Art Library/Natural History Museum, London; **137** Bridgeman Art Library/Private Collection; **138** below Jacqui Hurst (Lady Gibberd's Garden, Harlow, Essex); **138** above Andrew Lawson; **139** Howard Rice; **140** above Brigitte Perdereau (Erwan Tymen); **140** below S & O Mathews; **141** above Clive Nichols (Red Gables, Worcestershire); **141** below S & O Mathews; **142–3** S & O Mathews; **143** right Andrew Lawson; **145** Andrew Lawson; **146** above left Marion Nickig; **146** below left Marijke Heuff (Walda Pairon, Belgium); **148** left John Glover; **149** above S & O Mathews.

The following photographs were specially taken for Conran Octopus: Marianne Majerus courtesy of Dr & Mrs Cox, Woodpeckers, Warwickshire: **114, 130–1, 130** above, **131** below, **132** below, **133** left & centre. Marianne Majerus: **146** below, **147, 148** right, **149** below. Stephen Robson courtesy of Annette & David Beeson, Forest Edge, Hampshire: **54–5, 72, 73, 74-5, 128, 129** left.